Native Reading

Native Reading

How to Teach Your Child to Read,
Easily and *Naturally*,
Before the Age of Three

Timothy D. Kailing

An Elliptical Research Contribution (contribution number 2008.1)

Kailing, Timothy D.
Native Reading: How to Teach Your Child to Read, Easily and *Naturally*, Before the Age of Three / Timothy D. Kailing
1. Native reading. 2. Early reading—Education. 3. Child development—Biology. 4. Literacy—Education. 5. Parenting methods—Education. I. Title

Visit the Native Reading website: http://www.nativereading.com

For, and because of,

Freya and Otto

Contents

ONE

Introduction to Native Reading

I started reading to my daughter, like many parents do these days, from a very early age. But to be perfectly honest, Freya showed little interest in books and, in particular, she usually seemed to pay no attention at all to the text. So reading generally became one of those things I resorted to when I was tired of playing peek-a-boo or singing songs, or when marching around the house trying to get her to sleep just wasn't working. As soon as she got bored with reading, the book would be tossed aside, and I'd pick up a stuffed animal, or go back to peek-a-boo, or perhaps hand her off to her mother for a while.

My daughter was, without a doubt, more "high-maintenance" than her older brother had been—which was actually a bit of a shock, her mother and I had figured we would feel like experts the second time around—but she was still an absolute delight. As she grew into toddlerhood, it became clear that she was vivacious, funny, coordinated, clever (yes, I am a doting father!), and, also, more than a little stubborn, or, as I like to think of it, opinionated.

Freya was definitely a child who could not be pushed into doing something when she wasn't in the mood for it. Whether it was a new food we introduced, or a game she didn't want to play at the moment, or an unwelcome long car ride, she would often become what we called, *usually* with fondness, "contrary girl". So, when it came to reading with her, we did relatively little of it most days, especially when compared with her older brother, Otto, who had loved being read to at length from an early age. In fact, one of Otto's first words had been, "Again!" and it was very often said the moment a favorite book was finished, even after the second time through. With Freya, in contrast, the books were usually tossed aside, often only halfway finished.

Still, books *were* part of our daily routine, and she soon had a few favorites. As I'd done with her older brother, I nearly always pointed at the text when I read to her. This was a habit I had developed to an unusual degree. She never seemed to take much notice of my finger dancing over the text as I read: she was all about the pictures. Then one day, when she was about two-and-a-half years old, I was being a little lazy. My finger had drifted from the text and my hand was resting on the arm of our well-worn armchair when the magic word came, the word that I had almost given up expecting: "Point," she said, "Papa, point." Being the assertive little girl that she was, she grabbed my finger and moved it, not to the picture, but to the text on the facing page. "Read," she commanded.

This simple act, I already had reason to be quite certain, was evidence that a critical threshold had been reached—a sort of neurodevelopmental tipping point, to use a popular term. Within a few weeks Freya could recognize many words; within a few months she could read hundreds of words. Even out of the usual context of a book, she could read with confidence. She delighted in reading labels at the grocery store. When riding in the car, she began reading words from signs along the road. She quickly progressed to the point that—still before her third birthday—we could entertain Freya during road trips by putting a pile of books in her lap when we set out. She would sit in her car seat and work her way through them one at a time, reading them aloud from cover to cover before tossing them onto the floor. Many of these books were old favorites, and she was certainly using memory to help her reading. But from time to time I would also give her a new, previously unseen, library book. This was primarily just to surprise and delight her, but it was also to satisfy her skeptical scientist parents that her reading reflected more than a prodigious memory of previously read books. With only an occasional pause at an unfamiliar word, Freya would read through these new books nearly as fast as she read through her favorites; and she read through even these new books fluently, with natural intonation, and with clear comprehension, as evinced by her occasional comments on the action. Incontrovertibly, although she had not yet reached her third birthday, she was reading independently. She was reading so well, in fact, that it seemed practically effortless.

It so happens that, while we were certainly pleased by this development, we couldn't say that we were actually surprised. Her older brother Otto, you see, had started reading simple words much earlier—beginning at just eighteen months—and by the time he was two-and-a-half, he was a good enough reader to read aloud the entirety of *Charlotte's Web* to me. He did this over the course of a summer beach vacation because his mother had read the book to him earlier in the summer and he had liked it so much he wanted to share it with me. Otto's reading was so early and so fluent that he was considered quite a prodigy by many of those who encountered him. Most people were delighted. Some people were simply shocked.

There were also a few people—most often competitive parents with older children who were not yet reading—who were transparently *not* pleased when they saw Otto reading so well. Sometimes such a person would make a veiled, or not so veiled, comment about how they thought that kids shouldn't be pushed into reading early. While these negative reactions were definitely a bit unpleasant, comments like this actually turned out to be quite illuminating. You see, some of these same parents were people I knew well enough to know that they *drilled* their children with phonics flashcards, reading tutors, and other intensive means, all in the attempt to teach them to read. Yet their obviously bright five and six-year-olds were sometimes only barely literate, if at all. These parents were often palpably frustrated at their difficulty in teaching their kids to read, and it was clearly this frustration that led to their negative comments. For them, seeing a two-year-old fluently read through a chapter book…well, it kind of just rubbed it in.

But the source of their frustration, the struggle their children had in learning to read, is why I ended up finding these comments illuminating: because with both of my children, when they were each ready, learning to read had been almost *effortless*. My children learned to read just as they had learned to crawl, or learned to walk, or, especially, *just as they learned to talk*. They learned easily and almost miraculously. I can't really say that I *taught* them to read, they essentially learned it on their own, at the different ages where they were each individually ready. But both Otto and Freya learned to read at what most people consider an extraordinarily early age. And I don't think it is a coincidence that my early readers found reading relatively effortless, while many older children find it a struggle. Instead, I believe the problem is that most children learn to read too late. In fact, I believe that:

> The optimal time to learn to read is when a child is one to three years old, because this is the time when their brains naturally do the most closely-related task: learning to understand speech and to talk themselves.

4

Nearly all children naturally learn to understand speech, and to speak themselves, between the ages of one and three years (although the foundations do indeed start from early infancy). This is an enormously complex task, yet you don't really *teach* a child to talk. Instead, children learn to talk essentially on their own, so long as they are raised in an environment rich with speech and with social interaction. And children generally learn to talk with obvious delight, seemingly without effort and, often, with amazing speed. They don't learn to talk through regimented lessons, instead they learn by listening to and interacting with their family and friends, by singing songs, and by playing games. Nearly every child does this successfully, in every culture around the world, and children have learned to talk like this throughout recorded history and, surely, before recorded history, too.

Reading is different. I don't believe that learning to read usually comes so naturally to a child, *at least not the way reading is typically taught*. Some children certainly do pick up reading quite easily. But many other children find learning to read very difficult, particularly when they only started reading later in childhood. Some of these children even seem to actively resist the process, showing an aversion to reading when encouraged to practice. Such children can show a lack of interest in the subject, they can become easily frustrated by the quirky mechanics of the written word, some can show signs of dyslexia. The usual way people explain this observation—that some children learn reading early and easily, while others learn only late and with difficulty—is often by saying that some children are naturally gifted, or somehow more intelligent, and therefore they read early. While there may be some truth to this view in certain cases, I believe that, in general, this notion puts the cart before the horse in a profoundly misleading way. I believe that the reason some children read easily and early is because *reading early makes learning to read easier*.

I know this sounds strange at first. Most people consider learning to read a fairly difficult task. Look at how many six-year-olds struggle with it! And since it is difficult for many six-year-olds, they assume that learning to read must be much *more* difficult, if not downright impossible, for a four-year-old—to say nothing of a two-year-old! But this superficially compelling logic is *not* valid for all tasks. For example, nearly everyone now knows that learning a foreign language is *much* easier when you learn it at an earlier age. In fact, in general, the earlier the better. It is better to learn a foreign language early for the simple reason that early childhood is when our brains naturally are most receptive to language acquisition. It is a window of opportunity that, if missed, makes learning harder. You *can* learn a second language later, of course, but it is much more difficult to attain the fluency and accent that young children pick up with no trouble at all. Because of this, schools in this country have finally started to move foreign language instruction from the last few years of high school to much earlier in the curriculum, preferably all the way to kindergarten and even to preschool. Many people resisted this because, although everyone knows that children learn their own first language spontaneously and with ease in early childhood, they assumed that learning a second language would be somehow too confusing. The reality is, while there are occasional moments of confusion—moments when a child speaks a bit of Franglais or Spanglish—children generally deal with the additional complexity of a second language *better* when they are *younger*. Preschoolers, compared to older children and adults, are truly *geniuses* at learning languages.

Native reading is a new method of teaching children to read that makes appropriate use of this early aptitude for language. The core insight of native reading is that this natural genius young children have for learning spoken languages can, *if given the right environment*, be easily extended to written language, too. If children learn in this more natural way, they not only read years earlier, they also gain an ease and familiarity with the written word that is achieved by older children, if at all, only after a much greater struggle. Native readers learn to read as a natural, effortless extension of learning to talk. And the best time to learn to read this way is the best time to learn to talk: before the age of three. Better yet, when children learn to read in this more natural way, not only do they learn easily, joyfully, and at an early age, but they then become truly *native readers*. They become deeply and effortlessly literate in a way that has lifelong benefits, just as native speakers of a language have an ease and fluency that can generally only be marveled at by those who learned too late.

This is a very simple idea; yet it is also, in some ways, a radical idea. Are we really teaching children to read too late? You should be skeptical of such a claim, but that doesn't mean you should summarily dismiss it. If you step back for a moment and look at the big picture, it's really not so surprising that our current practices of teaching reading might not be the best. As I've just discussed, until very recently foreign languages were also typically introduced at what is clearly too late in a child's development. And remember, it is only in the last century or so that near-universal literacy was found in *any* country. So one cannot easily dismiss the possibility that we currently teach reading in a less than optimal way. We've only been working at it for a few generations, after all. Also, there is the additional factor that old habits die hard, including educational habits, and this is true whether they are good habits or bad ones. Consider, too, that children who have learned to read very young, while rare, are by no means unheard of. Many people have heard of a case or two of a child who could fluently read by three. Indeed, throughout history there is ample evidence that children are certainly *capable* of reading that young. For example, by the age of three the great mathematician Gauss could not only read, he also knew enough mathematics to correct an error in his father's payroll accounts! More recently, it has been reported that not only was the entertainment mogul Oprah Winfrey reading by the age of three, but that she was actually so fluent a reader that she started her career in public speaking at this same age, reading for her church congregation, to much applause and amazement. So reading this early is clearly possible for some children. But I believe that, *given the right environment*, learning to read this early, and this effortlessly, is something nearly *all* children are capable of, with their natural genius for language acquisition.

Remember, fundamentally, speech and writing are just two different forms of the same language. The critical factor is to create the right environment where the natural miracle of language acquisition extends to the written word. This book is all about the way to foster the type of environment that works. It is not a terribly long book, because the methods are generally simple and intuitive, at least once you fully understand what native reading is all about. Over the years of raising my children, I have compared the ways we encouraged reading in our home with the ways I saw other parents and educators try to teach reading. I have realized that while there are certainly many commonalities, there are also some important differences in method and even in philosophy. I felt that these ideas were important enough that I should share them with others. That is why I had to write this book. I have organized these learning techniques into *the correlation method of native reading*. If you use the correlation method of native reading consistently, and if you start at an early age, I believe that you can teach nearly every child to read easily and well by the age of three. I also believe that you and your child will have a lot of fun doing it, too.

I have written this book in the way, and in the order, that I hope will best communicate the important points of native reading, and I have worked hard to keep it as concise as possible (if you have kids, I *know* you're busy!). But for those who, like me, cannot always resist skipping around a bit, I'll lay out the plan of the book. The two most important chapters are Chapter 2, "The Correlation Method of Native Reading", and Chapter 4, "Creating the Native-reading Environment: 12 Techniques to Promote Native Reading for Your Child". In Chapter 2 I lay out the general method of native reading, and the logic that motivates the specific learning techniques that promote it. These specific techniques are then what Chapter 4 is all about. The reason I describe the general principles first and the specific techniques later is to emphasize that native reading is not a collection of particular techniques that just so happen to help your child read at an early age; rather, all the techniques are motivated by simple, but powerful, principles. If you understand these principles—if you really grasp the reasoning behind native reading—you can easily develop "customized" techniques that particularly suit your own unique child.

That said, many people find teaching by example to be the most congenial. If that is the case for you, you might even want to skip ahead and first read the specific techniques to promote native reading that are described in Chapter 4. In this chapter I explain each native-reading technique, I provide specific examples of using it, and in most cases I also relate my experience using the technique with my own children. After reading about these specific techniques you could then go back to Chapter 2 to get the general principles.

Chapter 3, "Learning to be a Native Reader is Fun!", is important because, given the struggle and the effort that learning to read can be for children who read later, many people have the misconception that learning to read is *necessarily* hard and that the process inherently involves drudgery. Understandably, such people want to spare this drudgery from a young child. Also, many people find it very hard to resist the faulty logic that since learning to read is often hard for a six-year-old, it must therefore be even harder for a younger child. Chapter 3 addresses these misconceptions and emphasizes that learning to read natively is, for your child, largely an effortless extension of learning to talk. You don't teach a two-year-old to read the way you might teach a six-year-old. In fact, the best way to teach native reading is through play, songs and, sometimes, through sheer silliness, because these are the things that young children respond to the best.

Chapter 5, "Early Signs of Success, Seeing Your Child's Progress", gives you some specific behaviors to keep an eye out for when raising your child as a native reader. It describes behaviors that give clear early evidence that your child is on the path towards native reading, even before your child is walking or talking. These signs of success are also important in teaching native reading because they indicate that your child has acquired skills that you can then respond to and build on, speeding and easing progress towards reading. Some of these signs of progress are subtle, and they also can represent "teachable moments" that are important not to miss.

Chapter 6, "Some Common Misconceptions About Native Reading", will hopefully seem unnecessary to you by the time you reach that point in the book, by which time I hope the logic of native reading has come to seem natural, and the benefits obvious. This chapter is included in part because you may find yourself encountering some of these same misconceptions when your child starts to read three years earlier than most of his or her peers. (That is, by the way, the only real downside to native reading that I can think of, the explaining you sometimes need to do.) Also, if you still find yourself a very determined skeptic after reading this introduction, you might even want to skip to Chapter 6 first—although I hope you won't read *only* Chapter 6—as it may address your questions and concerns most directly.

Chapter 7, "Can Native Reading Prevent Dyslexia?", presents the possibility that some forms of dyslexia may be *caused* by learning to read too late. I emphasize in the chapter, and I want to do so again here, that this explanation of dyslexia is no more than a hypothesis (that's why the chapter title ends in a question mark). However, I feel this hypothesis elegantly explains many of the specific problems found in common forms of dyslexia and I therefore hope it is given thoughtful consideration. This idea is potentially of such importance for so many people that I felt I had to include a chapter on it, speculative though it is. Because this hypothesis turns the logic of many commonly held beliefs about dyslexia rather on their heads, I expect there will be some who will find it controversial. This is especially true because perhaps the most troubling implication of this hypothesis, but also the most potentially important implication, is that many cases of dyslexia might have been easily prevented. The theory also helps makes sense of the otherwise confusing fact that dyslexia is, in some fundamental ways, a very *intelligent* disorder, and that many dyslexics are, indeed, extremely intelligent.

Finally, in Chapter 8, "What Native Reading Will Give to Your Child", I present what I believe are the essential, and life-long, benefits that learning to read natively will give to your child. Native reading is really not about simply reading earlier, it is about reading more easily, more joyfully, and with a deeper level of literacy. It is about making the otherwise troubling mechanics of reading so deeply *known* to your child that the technical, frustrating aspects of reading become almost instinctive, and your child is then free to better concentrate on the creative and meaningful purpose of language.

There is also a section of notes at the end of the main text. In these notes I have included more of the scientific details behind my reasoning, I discuss further implications of the theory behind the native-reading method, and I make some references to specific research and results that formed the intellectual background for my ideas. For many people these notes may present a level of detail that they would rather avoid, and if that describes you, you can just ignore the notes. I certainly don't feel they are *essential* to the text—that is, in fact, why I relegated them to a section of notes at the end! But if you are especially curious, and perhaps of a scientific bent, by all means do look them over. If you do, it may be useful to know that the notes don't need to be followed closely with the main text; many are structured as fairly independent essays and their purpose is to expand and explain ideas introduced in the body of the book.

Part of the reason I start this book on a personal note, with the story of my daughter learning to read, is to make something perfectly clear: this book comes primarily from my personal experience helping my own children learn to read easily and joyfully at what most people consider a remarkably early age. While I have been educated as a scientist, and this background has certainly inspired and informed my ideas, I am not a professional expert on reading acquisition. In general, I am a skeptical person, and I expect you to be skeptical, too (but this should also include skepticism of professionals, no matter how many degrees follow their names). But fair skepticism does not mean dismissing an idea without giving it thoughtful and fair consideration. My hope is that as you read this book, you, like me, will find that the ideas behind native reading simply make so much sense, that the methods become so natural and intuitive as a parent, and that being a native reader has so many obvious benefits for your child, that native reading will come to seem almost self-evident.

TWO

The Correlation Method
of Native Reading

Every child is a natural genius at learning languages in the first three years of life. Because learning to talk is such a normal and natural part of childhood, people often fail to recognize this process for the miracle that it is. It starts very slowly, beginning with essentially passive listening; only after many months does the seemingly meaningless babbling stage appear. From there a child progresses to the first halting words; not long after come the first simple sentences; and then, almost before you know it, your child is a chattering two-year-old who, some days, never seems to *stop* talking. Sure, young children occasionally do stumble on a few irregular verbs and they might garble complexly structured sentences now and again—and you may occasionally correct them when they make such mistakes—but they master the vast majority of the spoken language in an amazingly effortless process. No one has to actually *teach* them, rather, they just absorb the language in which they are immersed. They listen, they observe, they babble and experiment with vocalization, and after those first few words the process quickly "snowballs", building on itself. As the momentum builds, children soon pass a threshold where they quite suddenly "get" language; after that point, there is really no stopping them.

This process is so expected, and so entirely common, that it is hard not to take a child's amazing gift for language acquisition completely for granted. It is entirely normal, after all. But the genius of children becomes perfectly clear when you contrast their ability with the struggle most adults have when learning a foreign language later in life. We adults trip over all the irregular verbs, positively butchering the language. Sometimes there seems to be such a complicated array of tenses—the infinitive, the past perfect, the future perfect?!—that it can seem impossible to keep track. Practicing a foreign language can be an exhausting process; you can sometimes feel your brain positively *ache* with the effort. Then, after years of study, you travel to a foreign country and as you struggle haltingly in your second language, everywhere you go there are all these little children, the local children, hardly toddlers some of them, who speak better than you! It's foolish, but this experience can make the children in other countries seem almost preternaturally smart: "All those tiny little children *speaking perfect French!*"

One of the minor indignities of foreign travel is that this feeling goes both ways, but to reverse effect. Those tiny little children can find it positively hilarious when a completely grown up *adult* cannot properly conjugate the irregular verbs that they don't even notice. But this observation—their apparent obliviousness to the quirky complexities of their language—is a profound observation, and it is part of the explanation for their abilities: they *don't even notice* many of the idiosyncrasies of their language. They understand the language at a deep, native level that is almost entirely unconscious. Just as you generally don't notice all the irregularities of English ("I *am*", "you *are*", "she *is*", "they *will be*") because you learned these quirks of the language so early in your life that your grasp of them is, similarly, beneath consciousness. Your grasp is at a deep, almost instinctive level. By acquiring a language early, during that window of childhood when learning to speak is entirely natural and effortless, you gain a facility and fluency that can be matched later, if at all, only with extreme difficulty.

It is now well demonstrated that young children's natural genius for learning languages is so amazing that they generally have little difficulty even when they learn two (or even more) entirely different languages during their first few years. If they grow up in an environment where both languages are needed, their facility for language quite easily extends to encompass them both. If, say, their parents at home speak only Chinese, while their playmates at school speak only English, while there may well be a few periods of minor confusion during their development, before long they are typically fluently communicating in both languages. This is true even when the two languages are extraordinarily different in their syntactic structure, entirely unrelated in their vocabulary, and even when the languages have many entirely different sounds ("phonemes") which make up the language (think of the throaty French "r", the tongue-trilled "r" of Spanish, the "clicks" of some southern African languages, or the way that variation in tone carries meaning in languages like Cantonese). Like all true geniuses, not only do children master languages amazingly well, but they make this incredibly complex task look easy.

A basic insight of native reading is that the task of learning to read is fundamentally *easier*, if given the proper environment, than learning to speak two unrelated languages. After all, the spoken and written form of a language are deeply related; they are just two different forms of the same language, with almost entirely analogous quirks and regularities. So if nearly all children have the cognitive capacity to master two spoken languages in childhood, they are certainly capable of mastering the much simpler task of reading at the same age. The trick to doing this, if it can be called a trick, is to create an environment that naturally encourages the early acquisition of reading, right along with speaking.

The way to create the proper environment for native reading is to make a child's world rich in *correlations* between spoken language and written language. In this way, your child's genius for learning language is naturally and effortlessly extended into the written word. The idea of correlation is very simple, and children are absolute masters at picking up correlations. For example, it is commonplace for children to learn, even before the age of one, that hearing the garage door open means that Mama is home. Their mother might have been away for the morning, but as soon as they hear the rumbling noise of the garage door motor, they look at you with wide eyes and say, "Mama!" They can't see their mother yet, and they may not have the slightest idea of what's actually making the noise, but they know that when they hear that noise it means that their mother, if gone, is nearly always about to reappear. The noise is *correlated* with the appearance of their mother. Children get quite sophisticated at this and can pick up correlations we never intended to teach them. They may quickly learn that the phone ringing at a certain time of day usually indicates a call from a favorite grandparent. When they see you innocently take the sugar out of the kitchen cabinet they instantly put two and two together and shout "Cookies!" After the cookies are made they may show that they've learned that a particular sort of sigh you make, a sigh you were previously unaware of, means that you are about to give in and give them that other cookie they want so badly; hearing this exhalation, they may stop lobbying you before *you* realize that you're about to give in. Children are often so good at this sort of thing, it can be positively disconcerting for a parent at times.

This amazing ability to pick up correlations is at the core of a child's ability to learn languages so effortlessly. Even with very little explicit teaching, children quickly notice that a certain sound is associated with a particular object or action. By this means they quickly build their vocabulary. Children do not usually learn by being given an explicit definition of a word; instead, they learn by seeing the correlation of this word with aspects of their environment that are important to them, that pique their interest, or that are simply fun. They quickly move beyond single words; they learn that putting words together in certain ways corresponds to different actions or situations. After a few prototypical examples children soon learn to generalize this idea; they develop a sophisticated understanding of the ways the syntactical context of a word modifies its meaning. Very soon after this stage is reached, they are speaking in complex sentences themselves.

The previous paragraph is the merest sketch of the amazingly complex process whereby nearly every child learns to speak his or her mother tongue. Fortunately, to teach native reading there is no need to fully understand this incredible process. To help your child learn to read natively all you need to do is use some simple techniques that *consistently correlate the spoken language your child is naturally absorbing with the written language that is almost entirely analogous in structure.* The fundamental correspondence of written and spoken language greatly simplifies the process, because the correlations children need to learn are, in general, quite simple and easy to learn. Again, it is much simpler than learning two unrelated spoken languages with widely varying syntactic and phonetic structures. In fact, in many cases, the correlation between the spoken and written forms of a language is close to a one-to-one correspondence, which is the simplest sort of correlation that exists.

A good way to explain the correlation method of native reading is though the example of perhaps the most obvious and important technique: pointing at the text whenever you read to your child. I already mentioned the importance of text pointing in the Introduction (and it is Technique 5 in Chapter 4, "Creating the Native-reading Environment: 12 Techniques to Promote Native Reading for Your Child", where all of the techniques are fully discussed). When reading to their child nearly all parents point to the text sometimes, but in my experience almost every parent does this *inconsistently and explicitly*. They point *inconsistently*, meaning simply that most parents only very occasionally point at the text. And parents usually point *explicitly*, meaning that they try to actively turn their child's attention to the word to which they are pointing, to *teach* it to them. Then here is how it often goes: because most children would rather look at the pictures, they seem to completely ignore their parents' pointing, therefore, most parents soon stop pointing because it seems useless. The common sense feeling is that if most of the time your child doesn't even look at the text you're pointing at, why bother? And if you point at the text only on occasion, pointing probably *is* a waste of time—especially if you interrupt the story to do so, if you disrupt the natural rhythm of the spoken word that helps hold a child's focus, or if you try to force children's attention away from the pictures that they prefer to look at. Done improperly, it could even be counterproductive: inconsistent and explicit text pointing disturbs the attention of a child, it interrupts the cadence of the language, and it ends up making reading more confusing for a child—and a lot less fun. Text pointing improperly like this shows a fundamental misunderstanding because by pointing in this active way an adult is trying to explicitly teach reading to a child, and, in general, young children simply do not learn like this!

To transform text pointing into a useful technique you need to make a subtle, but crucial, change of method. You need to make text pointing *a consistent, accurate, but unobtrusive habit.* Pointing in this way, you do not actively teach your child to read; rather, this passive text pointing simply makes the correlation of the spoken and written words consistently apparent for your child, and this is all children really need in order to learn how to read on their own. By this simple change, by making a consistent habit of accurately following the text with your finger as you read in your normal cadence, you take away nothing from your child's enjoyment in reading books with you. But what you add is tremendously important: your pointing finger dancing along the text in rhythm to your voice makes the correlation between your spoken words and the written words on the page entirely obvious and natural. In a native-reading home, children do not need to be explicitly taught this relationship, it will just be a natural and obvious part of their world; they will simply absorb it. Rather than being a complicated new skill they have to struggle with later in childhood, reading is simply a natural extension of language as they have always known it. This sort of text pointing does require patience on the part of the parent, even a kind of faith, because during most of the time you and your child spend reading, your child will not be obviously following the text you are pointing to—which is exactly how it should be!

A useful way to characterize the correlation method of native reading is to say you are *mapping* the spoken language onto the written language. Just as a map is a model with features that correspond to the features of a landscape, the written language has features that correspond quite naturally and accurately to the spoken language. The correlation method of native reading is all about making this natural mapping clear and evident for your child, and doing this at the age when a child's brain is most effortlessly able to make these sorts of connections. By learning this mapping between reading and speaking in early childhood, children don't just learn to read earlier and easier—which in itself is certainly a wonderful thing—better yet, they become almost instinctively literate. For native readers, reading becomes an effortless extension of their fluency in speech.

Therefore, the foundation of the correlation method of native reading, and the motivation of most of the specific techniques given in Chapter 4, is to create an environment rich in consistent correlations between the spoken language and the written language. Some of the techniques also do something more basic, and something that many parents, having been readers for so long, can forget needs to be learned. *Children also need to learn to notice and distinguish the different symbols of the written language.* Again, you don't generally explicitly teach this to your child. In a native-reading home you simply make sure that your child sees letters and words often and early, you naturally incorporate letters and words into your child's play, and, importantly, you do this on a consistent basis. By doing this simple thing, children learn that these symbols are an important and meaningful part of their world. With this foundation it becomes perfectly natural for your child to be interested in the symbols of written language. Once this happens, given an environment rich in written and spoken language, your child's natural curiosity does the rest.

It is not an intrinsically difficult task to learn the 26 letters of the alphabet before the age of two or three, but this is not something that children do in most households today. However, it is commonplace for two-year-old children to recognize 26 different animals with no problem. And often these same children can go on and tell you the sound each animal makes! I once knew a four-year-old who knew nothing at all about reading—he did not know a single letter, and his parents were actually of the opinion that reading even at four was somehow impossible—yet this same child knew the names of what seemed to me to be *hundreds* of different Pokemon characters. And he could tell me all about their various characteristics and powers. The problem for this child was not that letters were so terribly hard to learn, the problem was that letters were not a consistent part of his environment. In contrast, my son knew all the letters of the alphabet soon after his first birthday. He couldn't *say* them all at first, as he was only just starting to talk, but if you asked him to find a particular play letter in a pile he could do it without a hitch. He knew them all because letters for him were fun play things; they were things to carry around, to throw in the air, to make songs about, etc. Of course, he also knew dozens of animals and the sounds they make! Learning to read early does not have to *displace* any other sort of play; as it turns out, it just modifies and deepens other play. My daughter, on the other hand, did not learn the alphabet quite so young—she had a *very* strong preference for stuffed animals and dolls when it came to play—but, still, just by growing up in a richly-correlated native-reading home, she knew all her letters by around two-and-a-half, and, for her, fully-independent reading followed very soon after this development. Though it won't happen at the same age for every child, in a native-reading environment, children will naturally come to see and take an interest in the basic units of written language: letters and words. When children develop this foundational knowledge early, the correlative techniques of native reading become very powerful and their understanding of the written word can then progress with amazing speed.

It is quite simple to summarize the basic reasoning behind the methods of native reading. First, by making letters and words a consistent part of their play from an early age, children learn to distinguish these units of language and they naturally become curious about them. Then, by making the home environment of children rich in consistent correlations between the spoken language they are already absorbing and the written language they are now naturally curious about, reading is transformed into a skill that children learn effortlessly, right along with learning to speak. By making your home a native-reading home, you make the simple mapping from speaking to reading an obvious part of your child's world. Reading is no longer a difficult task that presents itself later as an unnatural obstacle long after your child has already mastered spoken language. Rather, for native readers, reading is something that they have always known about, and their mastery of it, like their mastery of speech, expands effortlessly and naturally from a remarkably early age.

There is one simple detail I should mention, because it may not be obvious to those without a lot of experience with young children. While *reading* can come easily and naturally at the age of three or two, or even at one, *writing* generally does not. Fluent writing will usually come later for the simple reason that, for most children, fine motor skills are not sufficiently developed to support small-format writing (i.e., "staying between the lines") until the age of four or five or even later. In contrast, even two-year-olds generally have the fully-developed visual system and more than enough cognitive capacity to allow them to read easily, so long as their environment properly fosters native reading.

T H R E E

Learning to be a
Native Reader is Fun!

Before the specific techniques of native reading are
described in the next chapter, it's important to
emphasize one general point about teaching your
child to read natively. The point is simply this: native reading is
intended to be fun, and it is most successfully learned when
your child is singing, playing, and generally having a ball. You
should always keep this in mind when you're using the techniques of this book. For example, if at some point you find that
your child's interest and enthusiasm is flagging, it becomes
counterproductive to persist in any particular technique. It *is*
good to put effort into being patient and enthusiastic, but you
should never try to force matters. Learning to read should never
feel like a grind for your child. On the contrary, it should be a
joyful, creative and *social* experience, just as learning to talk is
joyful, creative and social. The techniques of native reading
subtly structure just a small portion of your child's natural play
and a small portion of your child's interaction with you. But
with this subtle structure, the techniques do something powerful: the fundamental correlation of written and spoken language becomes apparent, even obvious, for your child. And
when this happens something amazing results. Your child's
normal play becomes sufficiently rich in correlations between
spoken and written language and a critical threshold of natural

understanding is then reached. Beyond this critical threshold, reading is transformed into a spontaneous skill that children effortlessly acquire in the course of their play.

Native reading does require some preparation, persistence, and patience on the part of the parent. But from the child's point of view—despite the huge benefit of early and deep literacy—native reading amounts to a few fun additions to their repertoire of games and interests. To use a term from business jargon, with native reading you are *leveraging* your child's natural genius for language—the same genius that leads to effortless acquisition of the spoken word—and simply extending this natural ability so that it encompasses the written word, too.

I don't believe you can overemphasize the principle that learning to read can be, and should be, *fun*. It is worthy of emphasis because for many children who start reading later, either in school or just before, learning to read *is* a tedious and frustrating process. Many parents hazily remember this to be true in their own childhood, too. The problem stems from the fact that, from the point of view of a five-year-old, learning to read can indeed seem a chore, and an apparently pointless one at that. After all, by the time children are five they can already understand spoken language and, of course, can speak themselves, with essentially perfect fluency (notwithstanding the occasional lisp here or there). Suddenly, with the late introduction of reading, they are forced to learn an entirely different way to use the same language and, of course, at first it's both harder and less rewarding. It doesn't help that reading is typically taught in a way that's fairly asocial; often there is a comfortable but boring "reading corner" where children are supposed to "read on their own". But most children of four or five are intensely social and, until reading came along, language was always an exclusively and ineluctably *social* tool. Language meant talking with parents, siblings and with friends, it meant communicating wants and needs, and it meant playing games, listening to stories, and being silly. Suddenly, with reading, language becomes something you do on your own. In fact, if a child wants help from a parent or teacher while reading, it is often taken as a sign of failure: you're not yet doing it on your own, you need to work harder, go back to the reading corner and try again. (I should admit here that I personally have a clear memory of being scolded in kindergarten for talking with my best friend in what was supposed to be the *quiet* reading corner; I was told in no uncertain terms that I wasn't taking reading *seriously* enough.)

Given the way a kindergartner typically confronts reading, it shouldn't be at all surprising if, at first, children don't show much enthusiasm for reading stories *on their own*. Children would rather not struggle by themselves with mechanics like bizarre spellings and silent letters, with punctuation, and with capitalization. They want to hear a story at the same speed with which their already well-developed understanding can handle it. And children want to *share* the story with others. For many children reading alone is at first a slow, frustrating, and asocial experience. Therefore, rather than struggling by themselves, they naturally prefer to have *you* read the story to them. It is simply more fun that way; and it is the only way they have used language up to this point in their lives. Why let the drama and the suspense and the fun of the story get lost in these new mechanics of the written word? Why would they rather read by themselves, when sharing is so much more fun? When children are pushed to read on their own like this, it must often seem quite gratuitous, even a little cruel. Why are you making me do this?

In sharp contrast, native reading frees your child to acquire reading on his or her own initiative, in a natural and unforced manner. It absolutely does *not* mean somehow *pushing* your child to read. In fact, you are not really teaching them to read at all. Instead, what you are doing is organizing their environment so that reading comes naturally, just like walking and talking came naturally. By using the native-reading method you transform reading from a task that children typically learn later, and often with great difficulty, into something that they learn effortlessly, without really needing to be taught at all. Every native-reading technique is *social*, and every one adapts easily into the normal games, songs and other fun activities of early childhood. The techniques are designed to work most effectively at the developmental age when children naturally learn language the best, at the age of one to three years. In comparison, most children now learn to read several years later, when the developmental window of language acquisition is already closing. A child's ability to acquire language should be optimal before the age of three because this is the age when children naturally master spoken language—and remember, for countless human generations before just the last hundred years or so, spoken language was the *only* language a person typically learned. Remember, too, that just a few hundred years before that, nearly everywhere across the world, reading was something that only a tiny percentage of educated monks and scribes ever learned at all.

I believe it is this social history of reading, especially the relatively recent expansion of literacy beyond the most upper and learned classes of society, that accounts for why we still see reading as a "hard" subject, and why we introduce reading too late, when it is harder and less natural to learn. I think this history also explains why, even in these last few generations where literacy has been widespread, the occasional cases of children reading very early have been taken to be exceptions— usually as evidence of unusual genius—when in fact it makes more sense to learn reading along with talking. Just as people persisted in teaching foreign languages too late—and taught them explicitly, with boring exercises of conjugation, rather than through immersion—we still teach reading too late. Both foreign languages and reading have the social vestiges of being "advanced subjects" and people resist the idea that *children learn them better and more easily when they are younger,* despite the strong evidence for this.

The best method to teach a second language to younger children is through social games and play and, generally, through immersion. This way they absorb the language and learn its structure instinctively, with very little explicit instruction. Similarly, native reading is also best taught creatively and socially, with little formal instruction, in an enjoyable environment where children learn on their own initiative. It *does* require thought and structured technique on the part of the parent to create the properly correlated environment, but from the child's perspective the process of native reading really just expands the ways they can have fun. But by having this fun they learn to read early and with a deep level of competency—which is a skill that is critical to functioning in a literate world, both during their years in school and throughout their later lives.

Another reason that native reading is fun for a child is the same reason that can make it seem particularly effortless, even miraculous, from an adult's perspective: the fact that *native reading is a self-reinforcing process.* It displays what is called positive feedback. For example, even very early in their development, the native-reading techniques help children become familiar with the alphabet through simple *play* with letters. With this familiarity they naturally begin to notice the innumerable instances of the written word in their environment: on signs, on cereal boxes, on tags, even on the ubiquitous legalistic warning labels on their toys, strollers, and other kid gear. In noticing the words all around them, they become yet more familiar with the letters that were first introduced through play. They become even more interested in them, and this interest feeds back into their native-reading play, making it an even more powerful learning technique. When they develop the patience to read through whole books with you, their already established familiarity with letters, their knowledge that letters have names and are quite common in their world, will mean that they'll find it natural to take notice of the text in the books, too; this curiosity then makes your text pointing much more effective. All the techniques of native reading are *mutually reinforcing*. Just as with learning to talk—and using the very same genius for language young children have—once this self-reinforcing process reaches a certain threshold, there is really no stopping them.

So, as in learning to talk, the process often starts slowly and subtly but, once it takes hold, progress can be astonishingly fast, and gains its own momentum. With a little patience and persistence, before you know it you'll have a two-year-old singing in your grocery cart, delightedly reading all the silly brand names everywhere in the store, reading the nametags on the cashiers, and giggling over the vanity license plates in the parking lot. In the course of doing these things, during the mundane activity of grocery shopping, children learn new words, they learn how written language is used in their environment, and they are applying this knowledge to better understand their world, in all its variety. This is how native reading takes off for children, once you start the process. But, the point of this chapter is that, from their perspective, they are simply having a ball!

FOUR

Creating the Native-reading Environment:

12 Techniques to Promote
Native Reading for Your Child

This chapter explains, specifically and with practical examples, twelve powerful techniques that promote native reading for your child. If they are properly and consistently applied during the time when a child's brain is most receptive to learning the fundamentals of language, I believe these methods will lead most children to read by the age of three. It is important to understand that children will do this essentially *on their own initiative and at the time when they are ready*. Again, parents do not actually *teach* native reading; your job is to create the consistent, correlative, and stimulating environment that *promotes* native reading for your child. Then your child will do the rest.

The environment you create is one rich in correlations between the spoken and written word; in this environment your child's natural ability and inclination to understand and use spoken language takes over and extends itself into reading. It is your child's natural curiosity and joy that will lead him or her to master reading as naturally, fundamentally, and as *natively*, as possible—just as nearly every child miraculously masters the fundamentals of speech by the age of three years.

Remember, as the last chapter emphasized, none of this is meant to be any sort of academic grind for your child. Far from it. Trying to force the process would, in fact, be entirely counterproductive. Young children are driven by delight, by novelty, and by your enthusiasm. No young child should, for example, be sitting alone at a desk with a book of the alphabet. And unless you can somehow make it fun and interesting for a child, you should not be using flashcards to try to drill phonics into a two-year-old (maybe someone like Robin Williams could make it fun, but I doubt that the child would then be concentrating on the flashcards!). Perhaps such methods can work for some older children—those children who have already missed the optimal window for learning to read—but based on my experience with children, especially my experience watching my own children learn to read, I can't imagine such methods working to teach native reading. Regimented methods like that are, frankly, the way you'd teach a robot to read; and your child is not a robot. In contrast, all of the native-reading techniques detailed in this chapter are intended to be enjoyable and spontaneous activities for you and your child. You see, learning native reading amounts to just extending the fun of the early years of childhood into the realm of the literate.

While the process should always be fun, still, for a parent teaching native reading, it is very important to remember to be patient. Because native reading is not something that you can force on your child or rush in any way, patience is key. This is probably the greatest challenge for the parent of a native-reading child. It requires great patience to create the proper environment and then wait until your child is ready to make the leap to reading on his or her own, but that is essentially what you do. It is only after growing up in a rich native-reading environment for some months that your child will make the connections from spoken to written language, and will be ready to read. But when a child is ready, it can happen very quickly. Think of how a child learns to roll over, or how a child learns to crawl, walk, and talk, or how children learn just about any of the skills they acquire in the amazing first years. The process is seldom one of steady progress. Most often, at first, they don't even show any apparent interest in the task. After some time goes by they start to make halting attempts, which often seem hardly worthwhile. I loved, for example, the hilarious stage where my children, in their early attempts to crawl, went barely at a snail's pace—and *backwards!* Then, before you really realize it, *they are suddenly doing it,* almost as if they knew how to do it all along (and then you have to go catch them!).

That is exactly how my own children learned to read by the native-reading method. What follows are the specific techniques that help you to create a richly-correlated native-reading environment for your child, too.

Native-reading Technique 1. Play with individual letters, *consistently*, from an early age

Nearly all infants love faces from the moment they are born. As they grow older they soon love animals and pictures of familiar objects, too. But very few children show much early interest for the letters of the alphabet. Why should they? If you cannot read, letters are just meaningless little abstract scratches on a page. There is an appropriate saying in English to express this very feeling: "It's all Greek to me." Give it a try:

Θιβδος Γέφυίψες Ψόμραλ Χεδγβώάφχό
Φςαςυίθ Οοψρύιεσγτξδ Ψκβαφιόλέιζνεγ

Is it sense or is it nonsense? Unless you happen to have studied Greek, it's pretty daunting, isn't it? And the Greek alphabet is actually very closely related to our own alphabet, which means this is the easy example. Now try some Hebrew:

צְהוִי אפִי זאמזחקּסט ף שרְכֹלִי ףפוי זאבגדי

צְייזֹףיאכץ צזזק אמזץ דְףפדיזכליף זא ביגדזא

Or how about Arabic?

بــئ وَإِقَنْــزﻇﻌس بئــوإ منة تةثجذنــــة بــةأؤإنر

إةةعجذن ذنـإ ثـج قةبــةل ىقيحـد خةطﺎغف بــوإ

The point of these examples is that *this* is essentially what English (or any other language) looks like to a preliterate child. Abstract, meaningless, and probably frustrating to look at for very long. No wonder most young children prefer to look at the pictures in their favorite books and no wonder they generally ignore the text! In a typical home, a young child has no way of knowing whether such strings of symbols are important and worth looking at, or whether they are simply abstract decorative nonsense. (By the way, as a few readers may already know, the Greek, Hebrew, and Arabic examples above are, indeed, random nonsense.)

Therefore, the first step of native reading is to get your child familiar with the building blocks of written language. By introducing letters early and by making them a normal part of your child's world, you are demonstrating that letters are an important part of the environment, that letters have a name and a meaning, and that they are worth paying attention to. This is actually a *very* important thing to realize. It is not at all obvious to a young preliterate child that letters are in any way meaningful. It is something a child needs to learn.

Playing with letters *consistently* does not mean playing with letters all that much of the time. Letter play should *not* be at the expense of physical games, stuffed animals, silly childhood songs, picture books, or anything else your child loves. As with all the native-reading techniques, letter play is just an occasional addition to your child's usual play; and as soon as your child's interest lags, you should drop the subject. But if you engage in letter play just about every day, even for just a few minutes, you will make the fundamental units of written language a recognizable and fun part of your child's world; letters will be familiar at a deep neurological level. And remember, your children use your behavior to learn what is important in their world, so if *you* show them that letters are important, *they* will take an interest, and they'll soak it right up.

So that's the theory behind introducing letter play early. But how to actually do it? As always, the object is to be a little creative and to make it *fun*. For example, babies adore singing, so you can start by simply singing them the alphabet song while pointing to each letter of a brightly colored alphabet as you do it. With a toddler, a sillier—and therefore winning—extension of this is to sing the alphabet song, but to do it in your best Broadway voice, while simultaneously searching for the right letter in a box of play letters. Make a goofy, long and quavering pause in the song as you take a while to find the "E" that's hiding at the bottom of the box, with perhaps a dramatic, "*Finally*, the E!" inserted into the song when you finally retrieve it with a flourish. For good measure, start the song very slowly and then speed up gradually, so that by the time you near the end you are singing at a frenetic pace. Then with the final "*...next time won't you sing with me!*" collapse on the floor in a histrionic fit of exhaustion. Do this well, and I can pretty much guarantee you will be asked for an encore!

If song and dance aren't your style, there are many other options. Another good game is building towers with alphabet blocks, naming the letters your child sees as you build the tower up. You should narrate the action, saying things like, "Will the "B" block crash the tower?" as you put another block onto the precarious stack. Then laugh with your child as they come crashing down. If bath time becomes a favorite time for your child, those floating, sticking bath letters are a great way to do letter play. My son used to love to gather all the foam letters that had been scattered around our house since the last bath, and he would throw them into the tub as it was filling with water. He soon remembered the names of the letters that were missing, and yet to be found! We would go on a great search of the house for the last missing letter. The letters were a fun part of his play, and they already had *meaning* in the context of that play. They weren't just sitting dead on the page. In fact, finding the last letter and throwing it into the tub meant that bathtime would begin!

Play hide and seek with letters. Let your child choose letters to put onto a model train for rides around the track. Toss soft play letters for the family dog to retrieve. In all of these activities, be sure to *name* the letters for your child as you play. Once you try a few ideas, you'll find the games that are most fun and engaging for your child. As soon as children are able to grab things, using three-dimensional letters they can manipulate is the best—foam letters, alphabet blocks, those wooden letter trains that are made in Vermont—rather than just letters on a page or poster. Just having such tactile letters around the house is probably of some use, but it is *your* play with your child with these symbols of writing, your naming of them, and your interest in them that will set the stage for native reading. Consistency is more important than the sheer amount of letter play. If you make a big deal about letters for a week, and then let them drop from your repertoire of games, it sends a message to your child that letters aren't important anymore. But a modest amount of letter play nearly every day tells your child that letters are a normal, meaningful, and important part of the world. Rather than looking like Greek probably looks to you, the building blocks of written language will then be deeply familiar to your child, and through your play, these symbols will already begin to be correlated with the spoken language that your child is soaking up, even in early infancy.

Native-reading Technique 2. Play with words, *consistently*, from an early age

Right along with letter play, it is natural to also include word play from an early age. Go ahead and introduce whole words and read them to your child as soon as he or she is at all interested. A set of magnetic words that you put on your refrigerator is an easy way to do this; just make sure that they are big enough that your child can't eat them! It's even better if you can also find kitchen magnets that have pictures of the things named by the word magnets. You put the magnet of the word "CAT" next to a magnet with a picture of a cat on it and this sort of play becomes a powerfully correlative method (see Techniques 6 and 7 below). More generally, by *playing* with words, you are making the written language a familiar part of your child's world.

As always, much of the word play should be interactive, because children use *your* interest and enthusiasm to learn what is interesting and important in their world. But soon your child will also enjoy playing with these magnets, or other manipulatable word toys, entirely on their own. In the case of magnet words, they are also fun simply because they stick, they fall down, and when they do, they make noise. All of this is great. Self-directed play is also crucial to learning, even if it sometimes seems haphazard, or even "mistaken". For example, children may have fun turning the words upside down, side-ways, and every which way. They may sometimes seem to spend word-play time mostly making a mess of things, scattering their literate toys about the kitchen floor. You will probably have the urge to "correct" this apparently random behavior—for example, to make your child turn the words right side up—but you should generally resist this urge. Remember that teaching children to read natively is fundamentally different from teaching them non-natively at a later age. You should not intrude and correct them with a metaphorical "red pen". When children learn to read natively they will do a written-word version of many of the same things they do when they learn to speak. They will "babble" with their toys, they will enjoy nonsense words, they will, to an adult eye, spend a lot of time goofing around. This is not only all right, this is actually essential. Therefore, when your child turns all the words upside down on the refrigerator, do not "correct" this behavior. In fact, observe your children carefully, and you may discover that the time soon comes when they are consistently turning *every* word upside down, which means they already recognize the difference between right side up and upside down!

Just such an awareness of text orientation, in fact, was the first indication, other than his general enthusiasm for books, that my son was really on the way to reading at a very early age. When we would go out to eat at a restaurant we would entertain him, while waiting for our food, by handing him the menu, the little promotional cards, the dessert lists, the daily specials. We soon realized that he would almost invariably turn them right side up. He was doing this consistently by the age of eleven months, even when the items were nothing but unillus-trated text. During one family visit before his first birthday, one of my son's uncles was at first so skeptical about this ability—and soon so amazed—that he scrounged around for every piece of literature he could find, even several business cards, and, sure enough, Otto consistently rotated each one right side up, whether he was presented with it sideways one way, or the other way, or upside down. But remember, although Otto was already demonstrating that he understood something important about written language, he *was* a baby after all; so after looking at these items for a bit, he would typically throw the menus, business cards, and everything else on the floor, to enjoy the fun of watching Mama or Papa disappear under the table!

By introducing whole word play this early and consistently you are also doing something quite subtle for children: the hierarchical nature of written language, the way words are made up of letters, will become a natural fact to them, something they have always known. Also, a potentially confusing characteristic of an alphabetically written language like English also becomes a natural and normal fact. This confusing characteristic is the way that the same letter appears in different words, and even more potentially confusing, that very similarly spelled words can have entirely different meanings.

To be a little technical about it, the problem is that there are two largely independent levels of meaning of written English, with two separate "mappings". Whole words correlate with, or map to, semantic meaning. Letters correlate with, or map to, the pronunciation of a word. (To be sure, with all its silent letters, and with the multiple sounds the same letter can make, this can be a somewhat complicated mapping in the English language.) Fortunately, children are perfectly able to handle this sort of complication: the two levels of correlation are found in the spoken language too, so if a child is introduced early to letters and words, these two levels in the written language will come to seem as natural as the fact that, despite their different meanings, "cat" and "car" both contain a hard "c" sound.

Native-reading Technique 3. *Assemble* words from letters, to make clear how words are made from letters

In the course of your letter play with your child, now and again you should make a point to conspicuously assemble simple words from play letters and then read them aloud to your child. This combines the previous two techniques in a simple but powerful way. Also, by doing this you demonstrate that written language is a *creative* tool: the written word is not just dead on a page, or fixed as "atomic" letters which only have meaning when previously combined. You can *make* words from letters, and more to the point, your child can, too. Being as curious and experimental as children are—and with the insights provided by the other native-reading techniques setting the stage—even if word assembly was not clearly demonstrated for them, many children would eventually come to this realization independently during the course of their letter play. But when you make this process perfectly clear by demonstrating it yourself, you will help catalyze this breakthrough. Then your child will learn that written language, like spoken language, is not just something that you observe passively. Your child will learn that language can be something you *create*, and that it is possible to come up with novel combinations of letters and words that you've never seen before. Children love tools, and written words are a flexible tool that you can make and use to express yourself, to communicate. Assembling words may seem a simplistic form of this, but it's exciting for a child to learn, especially when you make the process fun.

You are likely to occasionally assemble words naturally in the process of working with Techniques 1 and 2, especially when using manipulative play letters. Indeed, it is hard for literate adults to avoid constructing at least a word or two when playing with a pile of wooden letters with a child. But making an effort to demonstrate word assembly with clarity and consistency during letter play is important. The simplest way to do this is to use a set of play letters and put them together, one at a time, to spell a few of your child's favorite words.

As always, making something of a production of this word assembly will make it much more fun and engaging for children. Name the letters and search around for each of them. "Where could the 'C' be?" When you find it, clear a space for the word and place the first letter with a bit of fanfare. As soon as children know their first few letters, you should deputize *them* to search for letters. "Could you please go get the big 'A' that's next to your wagon?" When they return triumphantly with the requested letter, give them an enthusiastic "Thank you!", and then set the "A" next to the "C". Go ahead and pronounce the partial word saying, "Ca, hmm, ca; that's not the word I'm trying to make. I must need another letter. 'T', the 'T'! That's the letter I need! Where *is* that silly 'T'?" A surefire hit is to surreptitiously sit on the last letter needed for the word, and get mock-frustrated at your inability to find it. Then, finally, you get up and act all surprised at its sudden appearance. "*There's* that 'T'! Good, now I can finish my word!" (Of course, if you do this last trick just once or twice, children will quickly catch on to the shtick, and then you can let *them* find the missing letter when you stand up, with anticipation and great delight at their success.) After this production, put the "T" down and read all the letters, then phonetically sound them out, then pronounce the word with enthusiasm. "Cat! *That's* the word I wanted to spell." Concluding with a search through the house until you find the family cat, should you have one, is a wonderful way to end this game. Just doing this sort of thing once or twice a day during your child's play, in a conceptually consistent way, is a very effective technique for teaching your child how written language works.

By the way, I give specific "scripted" examples, like the "cat" word assembly scenario above, for two reasons. The first reason is to make the technique perfectly clear, in practice, by being as concrete as possible. The second reason for using specific examples of native-reading techniques is that many adults find having a fairly scripted idea or two up their sleeves can really jumpstart play with a toddler. It's true for me, anyway. If you make use of one of these specific examples with your own child you should, by all means, deviate from the script when you happen upon a variation that's more fun and engaging for you and your child. Improvisation and varia-tion—that's the best. The specific examples here and elsewhere throughout the book need not, and should not, be practiced dogmatically, or without spontaneity. The *concepts* that the techniques teach are what are important. So the examples just provide a specific place to start. Personally, at the start of a long day with a child, I find having a "plan" for some of the day's activity very useful, if only as a fallback. Often I end up totally discarding the specifics and happily ad-lib throughout the day; but, if I run out of steam, I have a plan I can turn to. There is no denying the fact that enthusiastic play with a young child can be downright exhausting for an adult. Having a somewhat organized plan can give the more rigid mind of an adult a place to start. I believe that it is often a good idea to approach interaction with a young child like semi-improvisational music, where you start with a written melodic theme, and maybe you even specify the first few variations, but then you extemporize from there, once the process gets flowing. All the specific examples of using the native-reading techniques should be taken in this spirit.

An additional advantage of having specific "scripted" examples of native reading-promoting play is that your child quite likely has a grandparent, an aunt or uncle, or perhaps a babysitter who suffers from the disability of being "play challenged". These people may be entirely well-intentioned and may really *want* to interact with your child, but they often find engaging in spontaneous play with young children very hard to do successfully. This can be simply because of lack of practice, or it can be because they find the motivations of children just mystifying. Having a fairly specific plan of action can really help get things started for someone like this. And if you loan them this book, you'll find that play-challenged adults often find it much easier to motivate their play and maintain their enthusiasm when they understand how their "silly play" is actually doing something as important as helping a beloved grandchild learn to read!

Soon after becoming familiar with word-assembly play, children are likely to take this sort of play farther than you might have expected, and into directions you never anticipated. The fact that language is a kind of *tool* and the realization that *they* can make words is great fun once they get started. Nearly all children love to make things, manipulate things, and, of course, destroy things! So with word assembly, as with all the native-reading techniques, be sure to leave plenty of room for apparently "nondirected" play. This sort of play might appear meaningless to an adult, but it actually promotes essential intellectual progress for a developing child. So, as always, resist the urge to overtly "correct" your child when they experiment. For example, native-reading children are likely to pantomime the process of assembling words at some point. In their first attempts they may apparently pick letters at random, they may place them upside down or sideways, or even in a unorganized pile, and then repeat the last word you demonstrated. A child might place "MGQZAF" down very seriously, point at it and then say with enthusiasm, even with authority, "Cat!" You should not jump to correct a child when this happens, because this is one of those very special "mistakes" which are actually important signs of a child's progress and interest. Remember, native reading can start at a *very* early age, so when your child first makes a pile of letters and says "cat" like this, he or she might only be a year old. "Cat" might very well be one of the small handful of words your child can actually pronounce at this point. You can't expect your child to "get it right" yet. And it does no harm at all to do it "wrong" like this: just as babbling is *not* a wrong way to learn to talk, even though it is "nonsense". That children pantomime the act of assembling a word at all is the important thing, not that they get it right. The fact that a child has learned that letters can be assembled into a word, and that this group of symbols, jumbled or not, can correspond to a known spoken word—that is a truly momentous breakthrough. At this early point, the fact that a child might not know *which* word is really an unimportant detail.

Later, when children have much more understanding, doing things *intentionally* the wrong way becomes important, too. Not only is this okay, it's actually very good. Doing something the wrong way—and observing exactly how and why the way is wrong—is part of the natural learning process for most children. They often do this with language, just as they learn how their shiny new wagon works, in part, by dragging it around upside down, thinking something like, "Hmm, it *is* harder to pull this way. And look how the shiny red paint scrapes off all over the driveway! Cool!" (Of course, pulling their wagon this way also probably drives their parents bananas; this fact can also be interesting for a child. There is frequently an aspect of social experimentation motivating this sort of behavior, too.) So, in general, apparently chaotic play actually has a purpose, and when children play chaotically with words (which, thankfully, is seldom very destructive) you do not want to stop them. In fact, usually you should encourage them.

For example, as their understanding becomes more sophisticated, children are likely to enjoy extending word-assembly play to the creation of nonsense words—that is, *intentionally* creating words which they *know* to be nonsense. This is very different than creating nonsense words because of a lack of understanding. Like dragging a wagon around wheels side up, the usefulness of this sort of behavior can easily be lost on the goal-oriented adult, who often has difficulty seeing the point of doing things wrong. But, with a little guidance, such nonsense can actually be amazingly instructive. Both of my children went through a stage where they loved to assemble random sequences of letters and try to make me pronounce them. They knew these were not real words, and they found my attempts to pronounce them hilarious. They loved to make the "word" longer and longer and watch me struggle in my best attempts to pronounce "WEGTRYPZEDTRMSY". Then they would append an "X" to the end, squeal, "Say it now, Papa!" and giggle with delight at my even-greater struggle to pronounce the ridiculous thing. When my endurance for this was at its greatest, this game could, and did, extend to making a word that snaked halfway across the living room, using every letter they could find, of varying sizes and colors, with the end result a "word" that was impossible to utter without running out of breath.

Even with such a silly game, it's important to make it as useful to your child's learning as possible, particularly when making it useful also increases the fun. For example, a lot of adults (if they would put up with such a game at all!) might soon stop bothering to make any attempt to *accurately* pronounce such a linguistic monstrosity. It's just a bunch of nonsense, right? What's the point? But there *is* very much a point: by persevering in making my best attempt to accurately pronounce these random words, I helped my children learn two very profound things from this "meaningless" game:

(1) They learned that when they added a letter or two to the end of their written "word", which only changed the end of it, it was only the end of what I *pronounced* that changed, too. The beginning of the word, meanwhile, remained the same as it grew longer. This is an important correlation to learn.

(2) They also learned the important fact that the length of the written word correlates (sometimes quite hilariously) with the length of the word when it is *spoken*. This is another important and clarifying fact about written language.

Of course, they also got a great deal of practice in observing *which* sound each letter added to the spoken word, although I never belabored the point with particular phonic emphasis which would have held up the pace of the fun.

My son Otto found this sort of game such a powerful learning technique that one day, right around his second birthday, he came into my office and saw a television tuned to a financial channel. He caught sight of the stock ticker—the symbols scrolling rapidly across the bottom of the screen—and he found them positively side-splitting. For a thankfully brief period it became a favorite game of his to turn on the finance channel, then he and I would take turns trying to keep up with the whizzing stock symbols, doing our best to pronounce what was often only marginally pronounceable, until we were quite exhausted. He quickly surpassed me in his ability to do this, when his giggling didn't get in the way.

By the way, during this meaningless-looking and very unserious activity, my son showed clear evidence of remarkable comprehension, even though that was hardly the point of the game. Otto was born in the late nineties, so these ticker-reading games came at the tail end of the internet financial bubble. On one particular day that we played this game, some important news must have come out that impacted the manufacturer of the electronic Palm Pilot—a high flying stock in those days—so as we did our best to pronounce such nonsensical symbols as "MSFT" and "GM" and "INTC", suddenly a couple of "PALM"s zipped by. Recently we had gone on a family trip during which Otto had seen his first palm trees. Otto broke off the game, looked at me, and said "Palm! Hey, Papa, *palm!*" The way he interrupted the game and brought my attention to the *real* word amid the nonsense made it perfectly clear that he wasn't just mastering the low-level mapping of letters to sounds ("phonemes"), rather, even during this silly game of nonsense words, his reading comprehension was continuing to develop. Actually, it was the fact that my son *knew* that most of these "words" were utter nonsense (to anyone but a stock trader anyway) that made the game so funny to him. That and the way the letters zipped across the screen in such a bizarre manner. But to see a *real* word in this context, to see a meaningful word that he had recently learned amid all the nonsense—well, that was just *too* funny. I don't remember what that day's particular news on PALM was, but it must have been fairly significant because the trading was heavy and the ticker went by many more times. The ticker-reading game that day quickly turned into one where Otto waited for "PALM" to zoom by, and then shouted it out as loudly as he could, which was complicated by the fact that he was nearly dissolving in his laughter.

Native-reading Technique 4. Read books to your child nearly every day

Here's an easy one, as many parents do this already. Indeed, reading books to your child from an early age is a common recommendation today. Without the help of other native-reading techniques, however, reading even a great number of books to a child is not, by itself, sufficient to foster early and native reading. It is just not enough on its own. Still, the simple act of reading with parents is a very valuable *part* of the native-reading method. In fact, particularly when combined with the next technique, text pointing, reading books to your child nearly every day becomes an important part of the correlative environment that makes native reading possible.

One reason that reading to your child is such a good idea is very simple. Reading books is one of the dominant ways in which we encounter the written word (although computers are currently challenging this predominance). Simply by seeing books in the house, by being familiar with them, and by reading books with their parents, children naturally come to take an interest in books themselves. They learn to focus their attention and their curiosity on the pictures, the text, and the stories that books contain. This is a fundamental benefit of reading with your child.

It may seem strange but—even for the express purpose of fostering reading—some of the books that you read to your child can be, and should be, books with only pictures! If your child's favorite book is a picture book, do not by any means discourage that interest, and do *not* try to force text-filled books on your child. "Reading" a book that consists entirely of pictures of baby faces (often an early favorite) is still of great benefit because, even if *this* book has no words, most of the books your child will go on to encounter in life *will* contain words. So even if your child's first favorites are picture books, the important point is that he or she is still learning to enjoy books generally. Plus, your child is getting into the wonderful habit of sharing books with you. When children are ready, this habit will transfer to an enjoyment of books with pictures *and* writing, and eventually to an enjoyment of books that contain only text.

By the way, always remember that your children watch *you* to determine the important things in their world. If they see you throw a ball a few times, soon they will pick up a ball themselves and have a go at throwing it. If they see you using a hammer, they'll want to hammer, too. They may even "hammer" with the nearest thing to a hammer they can find—even a stuffed animal or a baby doll, if that's all they can get their hands on! Because of their imitation of your behavior and their observation of your interests, you can sometimes even help justify giving yourself a little break from the hard work of parenting. For example, when you're desperately in need of a break from active play with your child, if you take a breather by reading a book or newspaper in view of your child, you are *still* helping your child develop an interest in reading. Before long, they are likely to take a break when you do, and find their own book to read! It does, however, have to be kept firmly in mind that the value of such passive instruction has its limits, and it cannot ever substitute for interactive play.

There is also an upshot of native reading that I need to mention here. I've already remarked on the need to suppress your inner grammar teacher when your child engages in letter and word play (the strict inner teacher who has a red pen at the ready, itching to "correct" any mistakes or foolishness committed by a child during letter and word play). But you may also find that you need to suppress your inner librarian—the inner librarian who insists that all books must be treated with perfect care and respect. Children at one and two years of age are simply not capable of this sort of gentleness, not reliably anyway. In a native-reading home, children are completely familiar with books. Books are a normal part of their world. Books are therefore a normal part of their *play*, with all the potential chaos and destruction that entails. By all means keep any books you particularly treasure out of reach, and certainly you should teach children to respect and care for books. But this cannot be taken to the point where you find yourself constantly snatching books away from your children when they get too rough. It's important to have books that they can make into piles, carry in their wagon, or read to their stuffed animals when they tuck them into bed. If you have a hard time watching a favorite book spill off a wagon, get run over by the wagon wheel, and then get stepped on by your child, you might want to search secondhand bookstore bargain racks, or school and library book sales, and acquire a designated set of cheaply-purchased books that you can stomach being loved to death. Also, when books do get damaged, never underestimate the regenerative power of clear packaging tape.

Native-reading Technique 5. *Point* to the words, *nearly all the time*, when you read to your child

This is perhaps the single most important technique, as well as the most deceptively simple technique, in the entire repertoire of native reading. Pointing at the words is so common-sensical that it's something most people already believe is a good idea. Many parents occasionally point at the words when they read to their children. However, I believe most people have a subtly but critically mistaken notion of precisely *how* word pointing will help a young child learn to read. The result is that, in practice, very, very few parents point with the sort of fluidity and, especially, with the *consistency* that is necessary to foster native reading. Pointing every once in a while may well be better than nothing. Occasional pointing may help the brighter child towards at least an inkling of the higher-level, abstract idea that spoken words are somehow related to those strange symbols on the page. But what native reading is about is more fundamental; to read natively you must gain a lower-level, almost instinctive association of the written word with the spoken word, and for this *you need to point consistently and in a way that is not imposing.*

Remember, as I've already mentioned in Chapter 2, you are not trying to *make* your child pay attention only to the words. Far from it. Most children will be more interested in the pictures of their favorite books, and their apparent lack of interest in the text will make you tempted to stop pointing at the words. Resist this urge! The important thing to remember is that you are not trying to directly *teach* them to read—that's not how children naturally learn language—what you are doing is creating correlations in their environment that they will notice when they are ready. Children, with their growing and changing brains, are amazing at picking up correlations in their world, and the simple, intuitive act of pointing can do wonders to help them see these correlations.

Most people have a fairly straightforward notion of the purpose of text pointing. They think something along the lines of: I point at this word, say it clearly, and thereby I teach it to my child. In practice, the pointing and the saying are often done with considerable emphasis—and often to the detriment of the flow of the story. Also, there is a tendency for adults to begin *testing* a child whenever they make the extra effort to point at the words. They may pause in reading the story and point at the word again, trying to get the child to say it correctly on his or her own. Children being tested like this are often aware of the implied downside; they know they may get it wrong, and that they risk disappointment if they even try. Reading is no longer a fun and relaxed activity with a natural flow and almost musical cadence. Instead, reading like this, being tested at the whim of an adult, becomes a disjointed and pressured examination where the child is expected to perform. I think that most adults tend to test like this in order to justify the extra work they are doing by pointing; after all, why do the extra work of pointing at words if your child is not yet ready to read?

But the benefits of text pointing while reading to your child are much richer, more varied, and more subtle than this. When you point at the words, fluidly and consistently, as you read—*without regard to whether your child is even paying attention to your pointing*—the benefits start long before a child is ready to recognize even a single word. Even when children are only months old they will start to notice the simple but important fact that the rhythm of your speech matches the rhythm of your finger as it dances across the page. They will, at a very deep level, *expect* that the text and the spoken words are related. Many simple correlations will become familiar; for example, when there is little text on a given page, there are also few spoken words. You don't explicitly explain a correlation like this to a one-year-old, but with familiarity it will come to seem natural. And, like learning to talk, as this sort of understanding builds up through native-reading activities, the leap to independent reading eventually becomes a small and natural one for a child to accomplish.

With the search images for text that a native-reading child possesses as a result of consistent letter and word play, understanding can quickly go beyond this basic gestalt perception. Long before native-reading children are able to read independently, they may begin to recognize certain commonly-emphasized words. For example, my son was a big fan of

Beatrix Potter, and before his first birthday he could recognize the word "But" because so many of her pages start with this word:

"But Peter, who was very naughty…"

"But round the end of a cucumber frame…"

"But Flopsy, Mopsy, and Cottontail, who were good little bunnies…"

It didn't hurt that in our edition of *The Tale of Peter Rabbit* the first word on every page is also in an unusually large and bold typeface, which particularly draws the eye. Otto also quickly learned the words "The End". It became our habit, when we would reach the end of a book, for me to simply point at these two words, and my son would say them instead of me. I am not saying that he was actually reading at this time, before his first birthday. I am sure that, at first, he was using the stereotyped context of reading the story, and the auditory memory of my past readings, as cues for this sort of early "reading". But that is entirely the point. This is the way native reading develops. My son's reading did not develop in isolation from the natural way he learned to talk, or from the natural way he interacted with his parents, but, instead, his reading developed right along with it. His reading started out stereotyped and context-dependent, but it didn't take long to generalize. Very soon, just after his first birthday, he began to recognize and read his favorite words out of their normal context. And only a few months after that, he started sounding out novel words entirely on his own.

So your consistent and unobtrusive text pointing can help to develop natural and unforced reading in your child. For the parent, though, really getting into the habit of good text pointing—making sure you are consistent and accurate in your pointing, and learning to not let it interfere with your natural reading cadence—this is considerably more difficult than you might think. It is definitely harder than it looks. In fact, to be perfectly honest, it can be pretty annoying for a parent at first. Even after you do get into the habit, you may still need to fight a tendency to get lazy. As is true for all of the native-reading techniques, while text pointing does not require any additional work for your child—it just creates a natural correlation which children will gradually take in during their normal course of development—it does require significant persistence and patience in the parent. Until you're really comfortable in the habit of pointing and have learned to do it without thinking, you'll probably feel a bit frustrated. This is especially true because, for quite a while, your child will hardly ever seem to look at where your finger is pointing anyway! But by sticking with it, not only will text pointing become second nature for you, but it will deeply enrich your child's environment with an obvious correlation of reading and speaking. Because nearly all children have favorite books that they love to read again and again, there is a repetition inherent in this technique which makes it especially powerful for helping your child perceive the simple mapping between your voice and the words on the page. And grasping this mapping is natural for native-reading children because, with Techniques 1-3, letters and words are already prominent in their world, and they are naturally curious about their meanings.

While consistency of text pointing is important, this does not mean that it's some sort of catastrophe if you forget to point every once in a while. It is also perfectly fine to intentionally give yourself a break now and again, particularly when you're in the process of first developing the habit. For the last book before bedtime, when the parent of a young child is often sleepier than the child, you might let yourself off the hook, for example. So long as most of the time you are accurately pointing when you read, your child will pick up the correlation. It is important to be as accurate as you can be, without interfering with the naturalness of your reading. By accurate I simply mean that if your child looks at where you're pointing, you should nearly always be pointing at the same word you are saying. Again, this is actually considerably harder than it sounds, but, fortunately, accuracy becomes gradually more important as children get older. As your text pointing becomes, with practice, more and more accurate, your child will be making more and more use of that accuracy. For six-month-old babies, the pointing is mostly just a device that encourages them to take any notice of the text at all. At first, a child's perception is almost certainly of the correlated visual and auditory rhythms, rather than of the particular letters of the text. But you should not be lackadaisical about improving your accuracy because, before long, children *will* start to notice the particular letters and words and, if half of the time you are actually pointing at the wrong word, you will be making it harder for them. However, if you find yourself worrying so much about the accuracy of your text pointing that you start to avoid reading, or you start to slow down your cadence unnaturally, or you find yourself reading without intonation—*then you are worrying too much!* Do the best you can and, however imperfect, know that you are *still* enriching your child's environment with important correlations between the spoken and written word.

Native-reading Technique 6. Point, *consistently*, from the word for a thing to a picture of a thing, while saying that same word

So, you should develop good text pointing when you read to your child, but you should also point at pictures. Most children love pictures, and taking the time to point at pictures, and especially pointing from a picture to a word while speaking the word both times, is a simple and useful technique. Again, to some extent this usually comes quite naturally; many parents already do this now and again. The trick is to do this more often and consistently, and to do it from an early age. By *consistently* pointing from a picture to its corresponding word and saying the word both times, you are creating an environment for your child where the idea comes naturally that the abstract written word is a *label* both for the spoken word and for the more concrete visual depiction. Of course, you should also apply this same technique to the actual things themselves, not only to pictures of things.

Practicing this technique consistently will associate abstract written words with real-world people, animals, objects, and actions. As these associations become familiar, it becomes natural for children to begin to understand that written words have meaning. Quite early, a child will start using this technique on you, too. Once children become proficient at pointing (a skill which nearly always comes very early), they are likely to enjoy doing the pointing themselves. Both of my children learned a great deal, and thoroughly enjoyed themselves in the process, by pointing at words themselves and having their mother or me read the word to them. They especially liked those graphical "word books", where each picture is labeled with its name. My daughter would spend *long* periods of time doing this, pointing at the words and pictures while I pronounced them; she had an attention span for this that often surpassed my own. I'm sure that the way this activity allowed her to consistently manipulate my behavior was also part of the fun for her. (I also must admit that these word books' complete lack of narrative structure could sometimes exasperate me during the longest of these sessions, although I think I generally hid it well.) Soon, my children would also point out words for me to read on signs at the grocery store, the farmer's market, and similar places—it's not surprising that the word "SALE" was mastered early by both of my kids.

It is entirely natural that you will occasionally get tired of pronouncing words that your child points out for you. After all, for you, reading every sign in a grocery store is not a window into a whole new literate world. You may start to rebel against being ordered into action by your little taskmaster. Because of this, there's a good chance that you will be tempted to turn the tables and start pushing your child to say the word on his or her own. But, even when they are able to read independently, young children are likely to balk at this. Reading "on their own" is not nearly as much fun as interactive (and manipulative) play. Fortunately, there is a better way to both give yourself a partial break and to gently encourage independent reading: you should take turns. You read the word they point at, and then they read the word you point at. For both my children this worked magic when their reading was just starting. If I asked them to read entirely on their own, they would become self-conscious and show a great reluctance to read anything, but once they got into the rhythm of taking turns, I was often surprised and amazed at how well they could actually read—how well they could handle both entirely novel words and words that were familiar but out of their usual context.

Interactivity is, in fact, a general theme when teaching native reading: whenever possible you should make sure that the learning process is *social*. After all, language is fundamentally about communication; the native-reading techniques should give your child a new way to communicate with you and to play with you. While being a deeply native reader will certainly help children throughout their entire education—throughout their entire life, for that matter—long-term benefits are *not* what motivate a two-year-old. What will motivate your child is how *responsive* you are, and how much fun your interaction makes the learning process. When teaching native reading you should not attempt to make children "read on their own" for long bouts. In general, the more interactive your play is, the more enjoyable it is for a child, and the better your child will learn. Even when children progress to the point of easily reading on their own, interactivity should continue. When children become able to read whole sentences, take turns reading sentences in a book with them, just as you did earlier with single words. Long after my children could read very well on their own, they still enjoyed "turn taking" when reading books. Typically, we would alternate whole pages. I would often take the first page to get us started, and then my son or daughter would take the next, and we would continue alternating like this, until we reached the end of the book. Some people might view such turn-taking as a kind of social crutch, but I think the social "crutch" of taking turns is an entirely good thing. By making reading social and more fun, children end up getting much more practice. The result is that they progress faster, and more easily, than they would have had they been sent to some quiet reading corner to read on their own. And don't worry, in a rich native-reading environment, full of this sort of social reading, soon enough children *will* be reading on their own. In fact, when taking turns like this, both of my children would sometimes get so absorbed in the story that they would start reading *every* page without noticing that they had taken over entirely. When this happened I usually quietly let them continue on their own (while I was busy marveling, feeling full of parental pride, etc.). Upon finishing the book they would usually realize that I hadn't taken my proper turns, "Hey, you didn't read your pages!" I would usually make up for shirking my duty by reading another of their favorite books as a bonus.

While young native-reading children will usually prefer social reading, fully independent reading will appear when there is no social alternative. It can happen very early. In fact, on these occasions you are likely to be amazed at the extent of your child's reading proficiency. Both my son and my daughter did much of their early independent reading while I was busy driving and they were in their car seat with a stack of books. They would read away, happily amusing themselves, with much more skill than I realized they had. Once this stage is reached in native-reading children, in very little time they'll be reading independently just about everywhere, with no apparent effort at all.

Native-reading Technique 7. Label things from an early age

You should make a game of labeling your child's world, whenever a good opportunity presents itself. Labeling is another way of doing what the pointing of Technique 6 does: explicitly associating a written word with its object, and with the corresponding spoken word.

In practice doing this is very simple, but despite this simplicity, it can lead to powerful cognitive insights. For example, if your child's first word is "Mama," go ahead and stick a Post-It note that says "MAMA" on the appropriate forehead. I can pretty much guarantee that your baby will find this interesting. A young baby is not likely to "get it" of course; a baby will not understand what the written word "Mama" means for some time. But if you do this sort of thing with regularity, and if you have fun with it, you are creating a correlated environment where it *will* be natural for your child to eventually understand. Children spontaneously pick up reading through these techniques partly because a childhood full of this sort of play makes it deeply *un*surprising to them that there is a written word, in this case the word "Mama", that can represent their real mother. It accords with their early memories of the silly games their mother played with Post-It notes. It starts as simply a familiar association—which is certainly not the same as independent reading—but being familiar with the association of written words with real or pictured objects makes the leap to true reading a much smaller and more obvious step.

For another example of labeling, when your child is playing with bath letters in the tub, go ahead and spell "BATH" right there, while they are in the midst of it. Another easy way to incorporate labels is to make a game of putting nametags on all their favorite stuffed animals, perhaps on the formal occasion of a stuffed animal tea party. With this simple addition, social play-acting becomes a way to learn reading, too.

I am definitely not the artist of the family, but my children loved it when their mother, who can sketch quickly and beautifully, would draw a bear, or a frog, or a wolf right before their eyes. When she did this, she generally printed a label next to each animal, too. Again, the simple and unobtrusive addition of labeling during these drawing sessions turned it into effective native-reading play, too.

It *is* a bit artificial and simplistic to stick tags on everything, and for this reason I don't think overdoing labeling is warranted. In fact, if one *really* went overboard with labeling, it might be possible for a child to learn language a bit too inflexibly, perhaps missing some of the nuance and social subtleties that are an intrinsic part of language. A child might come to expect meaning to be as explicitly clear as a label, when it generally has to be figured out from a more complex social and environmental context.

But, when not taken to the extreme (and, to be clear, I think "extreme" labeling would entail a virtual snowstorm of Post-It notes, covering your home in drifts), labeling, by making the association of a written word and its object crystal clear, is a very valuable native-reading technique.

Native-reading Technique 8. Show your child his or her own name in letters

This is a very short and simple auxiliary technique. It is, of course, a specific variant of labeling, but it deserves separate treatment because it can be so particularly effective. Children have a natural interest in their own name, so when playing with words (Technique 2), assembling words (Technique 3), and using labels (Technique 7), be sure to include your child's own name in the play. For both of my children, their given name was one of the first words they could recognize easily, even in an unusual context.

Children are likely to be fascinated with the names of their family members and close friends, too. So, in the course of early native-reading play, you should also introduce your child to the words "Mama" and "Papa" (or "Mommy" and "Daddy", or whatever your child typically calls you), and similarly introduce the names of their siblings, favorite cousins, family pets, or whoever else is important in your child's social world.

Because your child is so familiar and fluent with the spoken form of these words, these are likely to be the first words for which your child really "gets" the correlation with the written form of the word. In fact, native-reading children are likely to begin recognizing a few written words at *such* an early age that you need to be careful not to get your expectations *too* high. Because the native-reading techniques make children deeply familiar with letters and words, they will typically recognize and understand a few favorite *prototypical* written words very early, long before a *general* understanding of the correlation of spoken and written language is reached.

As with much of their development, while children certainly do eventually arrive at general cognitive rules, they don't usually start with the general rules, not at the very outset. Typically children start by learning specific examples first; they then go on to use this anecdotal experience to arrive at a generalization, *inductively* producing a more universal model. The generalized model can then be used to extrapolate from their experience. This allows them, for example, to deductively arrive at a past tense of a less common verb from the rule they generalized from other more familiar verbs (this is why children typically go through a stage where they say things like "I swimmed yesterday", which is one of the "mistakes" that actually shows their genius in action). The important point here is that deep understanding seldom starts with the general rule; first come the specific examples, which act as prototypes. Only later will the commonalities of these specific memories be distilled into general understanding. In children's progress towards native reading, their own name and the names of the ones they love serve wonderfully as these prototypes of experience.

Native-reading Technique 9. Introduce uppercase *and* lowercase letters

In all your reading with your child and in your various letter and word play you should not be afraid to use uppercase *and* lowercase letters. In fact, I believe uppercase and lowercase letters should both be introduced *early* in reading play. Children will see both sorts of letters throughout their life, and the earlier they become familiar with quirks of written language like capitalization the more natural they will seem. At the same time, there is no need to go out of your way to introduce cases; rather, just allow the introduction to come naturally. So long as you are not actively oversimplifying the written language you introduce to your child, uppercase and lowercase letters will end up being encountered in the same natural way that they appear in the written world.

There *is* a tradeoff here. It's not a bad idea to simplify written language to a certain degree. In fact, for the spoken word, nearly all parents instinctively use "babytalk" with infants, which generally simplifies speech and also exaggerates some of its most important features. In practice, given the typically available resources for parents, it is actually difficult to avoid moderate simplification of a child's early exposure to the written word. For example, many early children's books use only capital letters, most letter playsets have no lowercase letters, and many alphabet blocks are also uppercase only. The degree of simplification this provides is generally fine and to some extent it's useful. But it is important not to overdo this sort of thing. You should not take such simplification as an overarching rule and you should not *over*simplify the language by, for example, completely avoiding all lowercase letters until a child is a fully fluent reader. If you do this your child *might* possibly read slightly earlier, but your child will also become accustomed to artificially homogeneous writing that does not accurately reflect the writing that she or he will encounter throughout life.

Again, remember that your two-year-old child really is a genius at these sorts of complexities. They are *much* more capable than you, to be a bit brutal on your ego. Young children are extraordinarily adept at picking up complications and quirks of language and using them as if they were perfectly natural. Let them use their genius; don't shelter them from the complexity that they can handle particularly well at this age. For example, in helping your child learn to speak you should never allow your babytalk to go to the extreme of saying things like "Baby eated the food," or "Mama beed at work yesterday," or "You haved a good nap." Speaking like this, regularizing the irregular language, gives children an oversimplified and downright misleading example of proper speech. Children raised in such an environment would have to learn everything *twice* that way, if they could manage at all to unlearn the wrong way they were first taught. Now, it is a very different thing if your child independently says "I eated enough already." I don't believe more than a gentle correction, if any, is called for when this happens. But when children make little stumbles like this, you also don't want to *reinforce* their misunderstanding of language by saying it wrong yourself.

With native reading you take an analogous approach (this should be unsurprising since native reading relies on the very same cognitive strengths young children use to master speech). So, if your child prefers to use capital play letters first, you shouldn't go out of your way to emphasize lowercase letters, in an attempt to correct this preference. But neither should you cater to their limitations by taking pains to avoid lowercase letters. This same approach to uppercase and lowercase letters also applies more generally to the various fonts of printed words, and even to cursive. In general, you shouldn't exaggerate the complexities, but you also shouldn't go out of your way to shelter your child from the natural diversity of the written word.

In practice, children are so incredibly good at learning to see what is essential, and at learning to ignore what is not essential, that any preference or limitation they show, say, for capital letters or for simple fonts, is likely to be very brief. My son learned his letters very early, in the form of simple, sans-serif, capital-only bath letters. With my limited adult brain, I was *sure* he would have serious difficulty generalizing his knowledge. He had a small indoor jungle gym with spinning letter blocks on it. These letters were capitals, too, but for some reason they were in a very stylized, angled and curlicued font. I felt certain that Otto wouldn't recognize *these* bizarre versions. But when I tried him, pointing at each of the almost-inscrutable letters, he sang out their names without the slightest mistake or hesitation. For a few weeks he was less sure about the lowercase letters. But again, without any particular effort, and probably mostly from the passive activity of reading and text pointing, he very soon mastered all the lowercase letters, too. With my daughter, who read somewhat later than my son, the process was subtler, but in some ways more impressive. Freya's understanding didn't show much at all in the way of discernable stages. Before the age of two-and-a-half she wasn't enthusiastic about identifying letters, and in general she showed relatively little understanding of written words. She did know the alphabet by around the age of two, and she definitely recognized her own written name, her brother's name, "Mama" and "Papa", "Cat" and sometimes "Dog", and a few others. But that was about it, really. Then, in just a few months starting when she was two-and-a-half, her understanding rapidly expanded to include lowercase letters, whole words, and fully-independent reading—even reading her parents' cursive writing. Actually, both of my kids learned to read my cursive writing so quickly that I can't actually recall them *not* knowing how to read it, despite the fact that I never won any awards for penmanship. Both my son and daughter went through a phase where they insisted on holding the grocery list when shopping; their ability to read cursive writing was obvious in the way they would call out the items on the scrawled grocery list, as they sat in the cart and happily kicked their feet.

Native-reading Technique 10. Play rhyming games, with both spoken words and written words

Children love rhymes. Such "child's play" is not only fun—it's actually an amazingly insightful way of exploring language. With rhyming play, along with the fun, a great deal of cognitive work is getting done, too, and it is getting done in a very efficient manner. It may not be immediately apparent to most adults, but when children play around with rhymes, they are intuitively acting very much like rigorous scientists of language. Your little language researcher is actually performing controlled experiments with words during rhyming play. It looks like fun (and it *is* fun!) but by holding the end of the word constant and varying only the beginning, children can isolate and focus their attention on just the part of the word that changes. So, by playing rhyming games with your children, you will not only delight them, you will also act as their research assistant in their silly, but seriously effective, experimental studies of communication. This makes playing rhyming games a great way to help a child sail along towards native reading.

By comparing "CAT" and "HAT", for example, whether in speech or in writing, children can focus their attention on just one part of each word—one "phoneme" of the spoken word, which generally correlates with one letter of the written word (or just a few letters, for phonemes like "th" and "sh"). At the same time, the rest of the word is held steady. Instead of trying to master the "C", the "H", the "A", and the "T", a child can just focus on the different effects the "C" and "H" have. To be sure, during such play children are also passively reinforcing whatever knowledge they already have of the pronunciation of the other letters, and of the whole words, too. But they are concentrating on just the first sounds and letters. This is a brilliant technique for learning language.

Speaking of cats and hats, rhyming books are, like rhyming play in general, a favorite of children for the same good reasons. So by all means indulge your child's pleasure in Dr. Seuss and other seriously silly authors. Rhyming books also serve as a wonderful way to get creative word play started. For example, my children were usually instantly engaged and delighted if I started play with a story they already knew, but then took it in a new and unexpected direction, using the rhyming scheme as my guide. For example, you might start a story with the title character of Dr. Seuss's *The Cat in the Hat*, but then tell your own new story where the Cat meets a Rat with a Bat who ate the Cat's Hat and, as a result, became rather Fat...and so on.... Along the way you should encourage your children to come up with a rhyming word of their own and then see in what ridiculous directions it takes the story. Of course, this sort of activity does much more than helping develop native reading, it also helps children increase their spoken vocabulary, lets them practice their pronunciation, starts developing their sense of narrative, and it gives them a facility with taking turns, among other skills.

The effectiveness of this play is greatly enhanced—and the correlation of written and spoken words is made much more plain—if you use your child's play letters to assemble the rhyming words in written form (that is, incorporate word assembly, native-reading Technique 3, into this rhyming game). This can also help you find new rhymes when you begin having difficulty coming up with new ones in your head. So start with the letters laid out to spell "CAT", remove the "C" and replace it with an "H" as you get to that word, then replace the "H" with the "R" when the rat enters your version of the story, and so on. Your child will pick up the logic very quickly and this play becomes naturally interactive; by all means encourage your child to find a new letter for you and try to make this new rhyming word fit into the story. That some of the resultant "words" will be completely absurd nonsense is just part of the fun, just the way nonsense words are part of the delight of Dr. Seuss books.

By the way, there is another literary technique called "alliteration" that, while somewhat less familiar than rhyming, is also a very effective basis for this sort of word play. Alliteration is the poetic device where words *start* with the same sound, so it's sort of the converse of rhyme. For example, alliteration is found in the following phrase: "the bit, burnished bright and broad at the edge", which is a line from the anonymous fourteenth century poem "Sir Gawain and the Green Knight". (Alliterative poetry was formerly very common in English literature, but the fashion has fallen from favor and, indeed, alliteration tends currently to be considered quite cloying.) With alliterative play the beginning of the words are held constant and children can focus their attention on just the variable end of the word. Between alliteration and rhyme your little scientist of language can carry out linguistic experimentation from both ends of a word. The same sort of story games just described for rhyming can be done with alliteration, although with alliteration the work of finding and arranging letters is often a bit more difficult. This is because, typically, more letters must be exchanged to change from one alliterative word to another than is usually the case with short rhyming words. However, as long as you're up to the challenge, this increased difficulty—which may force you and your child to madly scramble about in search of the right letters—ends up making the play just that much more silly and fun for your child, albeit somewhat exhausting for you. By the way, many children's books do make some use of alliteration, although most people don't notice it as consciously as they notice rhyming.

It may have occurred to you that there are some potential confusions that may arise in the course of rhyming and alliterative games. For example, not only do "huff" and "puff" rhyme, but so does "rough". And "not", "knight", and "gnome" all start with the same sound. This is because the mapping of letters and sounds in English, as with most languages, is not a simple one-to-one mapping. There are exceptions to most rules and there are redundancies to the rules. In general I believe you should *not* avoid these complications. There is a natural and well-meaning urge to artificially simplify the language to make it easier for your child to comprehend, but I think this should usually be avoided. Children have a quite amazing ability to see complex conditional relationships and I think oversimplification can do more harm than good. Now I'm not saying you should go out of your way to find hard words, playing your first rhyming game with "key", "tea", "lee", and "quay", for example. But if you *over*simplify the real complications of language, children may then learn in an artificially inflexible way. Later such children could struggle with the many exceptions in natural language, which would then seem unexpected, surprising, and frustrating. As with capitalization, I believe that a fairly "neutral" approach is the best course of action: don't exaggerate complexity, but don't oversimplify either. If children encounter the exceptions and complications of language in a natural manner, at the same rate they will actually encounter them throughout their life, they will learn these complexities most instinctively. These exceptions, just like the many common irregular verbs in speech, will become deeply familiar to them. The understanding they develop will then tend towards a perfect match: just as flexible, and as inflexible, as the language itself.

So playing games with both alliteration and rhyme helps a child see the structure and mechanics of language, in both the written and spoken form. When you include letter play and word assembly, these poetic games become particularly effective native-reading techniques—as well as particularly fun techniques. These games make the correlation of letters and sounds, and the correlation of whole written and spoken words, increasingly familiar and intuitive for your child. It is no wonder that children are such spontaneous geniuses at language; the way they love to experiment with words shows that, when it comes to language, they are natural scientists *and* natural poets.

Native-reading Technique 11. Use music and song to aid early reading

With a little ingenuity a parent can use a young child's love of song to promote native reading, as well as to simply have fun. We already had an example of this during the discussion of letter play (Technique 1) when I suggested performing your best Broadway version of the ABC song, while illustrating the song with the appropriate play letters. Song is such a wonderful way to engage a child I'm surprised it is not used more systematically to help learning throughout childhood.

Like the alliteration and rhyme of the previous technique, music helps guide and structure play, which is wonderful for children, and which also can be helpful for play-challenged adults. Of course, the simple fact that nearly all children love to sing is the main advantage of incorporating music into your play whenever you can. It's also important because music clearly helps structure memory. Many children who have difficulty memorizing phrases, or even short poems, nevertheless can recall many classic children's songs in their entirety, once they get going. Music has a momentum that is similar to the momentum children must learn to generate themselves in order to read complex sentences with fluency and comprehension.

Using music during native-reading activities is simple to do. Singing the ABC song during letter play is already one example. You can play a similar game with "Old McDonald had a Farm" by pointing at pictures of each animal as you sing it with your child the first time through, then, during the encore performance, you can point at the written words for each animal as you sing each name out.

If your child has a recording of favorite children's songs, print out the lyrics so that you and your child can sit in a comfortable chair and read along, with text pointing, while you listen to the music. Because of the momentum and flow of music—the way the words of a familiar song spring almost magically to mind along with the tune—your child will not just be *hearing* the words on the recording but will also be *recalling* the words. Children will anticipate the arrival of the next words and phrases of the song and then feel them dovetail into the music in a way that feels cognitively right. I believe that reinforcing this sort of cognitive rhythm can carry over into the music-like fluency that characterizes a truly good reader. We sing before we speak.

Native-reading Technique 12. If at all possible, breastfeed your child

I don't believe that breastfeeding your child is necessary in order for your child to read natively. I do, however, think it is a very good idea.

Whether breastfed or not, nearly every child learns to talk before the age of three, and native reading, which makes use of this same natural language ability, should similarly be possible for the formula-fed child. However, native-reading children do have a wider world to make sense of, as they join the literate world, too. Also, the correlations between the written and spoken word that children must learn to recognize are fairly subtle and abstract (although the native-reading techniques make these correlations as clear and concrete as possible). Because of this, parents who are raising native readers will certainly want to support their children's brain development as best as they can. As in all areas of intellectual development, giving children the full neural resources that breastfeeding naturally helps develop is clearly a good idea.

Of course, the recommendation of breastfeeding is certainly not specific to native reading. As the saying goes: breast is best. Breastmilk is clearly the best and most natural food for a human infant, and scientific research confirms that it best promotes early brain development. In fact, formulas unsupplemented with docosahexaenoic acid (DHA) are, in my opinion, and in the opinion of many nutritional experts, frankly deficient when it comes to supporting brain growth. DHA is an omega-3 fatty acid which is critical for brain growth and function and which is, no coincidence, plentifully supplied by breastmilk. But even supplemented formulas have none of the immunological benefits, or the adaptive, changing composition as your baby grows, that come naturally with breastmilk.

But, again, to be clear, I am not saying that a formula-fed baby cannot become a native reader; what I *am* saying is that it is biologically and medically clear that the best environment to promote native reading, as with all other cognitive development, includes being breastfed.

These are the twelve specific techniques that make up the correlative method of native reading. Each technique helps to create an environment rich in correlations between spoken and written language for your child. In this correlated environment reading develops early, deeply, and effortlessly, as a natural extension of learning to speak. After reading the descriptions of the techniques I hope that they already feel like perfectly straightforward methods to you, and that you find them useful additions to your child's play. Again, they are just *additions*. The native-reading techniques need not, and should not, replace any of the natural play of your child. Peek-a-boo, patty-cake, games of chase, and all the rest should be enjoyed whole-heartedly. Of course, as it turns out, because nearly all play includes speaking or singing, in a native-reading home a great proportion of normal play *will* naturally promote reading, because native-reading children become so deeply literate. When a child starts to "get" the mapping between spoken language and written language very early in life, there is no competition between the two forms of communication at all. When children are raised as native readers, everything that encourages learning to talk also helps them on the road towards reading. When they hear a new word, the image of its written form comes easily to mind, because the mapping from sound to symbol becomes so intuitive for them. Soon enough, this will work in the other direction, too: when native readers become fluently-reading three-year-olds, everything they read will also help reinforce the sophistication of their speech. It becomes mutually beneficial to learn to speak and read at the same time.

It should be obvious from their description, but I want to state clearly that the native-reading techniques are not meant to be used separately. Actually it can be quite difficult to do so, and it would be counterproductive to try to keep the techniques artificially separate somehow. The techniques are best used in natural combinations. For example, if you sing the alphabet song while finding and arranging play letters along with the lyrics, you are combining Technique 1 and Technique 11. Or if you and your child sing a favorite song, while following and pointing at the lyrics in a children's songbook, you are combining Techniques 4, 5, and 11. This is all good. Just pay close attention to your child and remember that you *should* customize your application of the techniques, both for your child's particular personality and for your child's changing abilities and interests at each stage of development. There is no simple rule for this because every child responds differently— my children were certainly quite different from each other. Just use children's interest and attention, and their delight, to guide your unique implementation of the techniques.

Friends, relatives, and teachers—who have often been amazed at how early and how well my children could read— have frequently asked me how many minutes or hours a day we spent reading to them. It's a surprisingly hard question to answer. Their mother and I never punched a time clock, and we never had any particular daily regimen, other than a practice of stories at bedtime. The best answer is in two parts. First, we used native-reading techniques *consistently*; that is, we used at least one or two of the techniques with our children, even if only briefly, nearly every day. Second, the duration of our native-reading play was for as long as our children enjoyed it each day—or at least as long as our schedules allowed, and as long as *our* energy held out. Some days, perhaps a day spent playing in the year's first snow, or during a busy family vacation, our native-reading time might only amount to reading our children a book or two while text pointing. But there were also days, especially days when our children had recently reached a critical threshold of understanding, where they were *very* enthusiastic and wanted to spend long sessions engaged in native-reading play. At these times they would sometimes spend much of the day assembling their own words, or pointing at words in a book while a parent pronounced them, or simply reading many, many books and reminding us to "Point!" if we ever got lazy with the text pointing. Being able to participate in the occasional "learning marathon" like this is wonderful, and at these times, when a child is ready and eager to learn, the progress that can be made is amazing. But, in general, if you consistently spend just half an hour a day using native-reading techniques I believe you can firmly establish your child on the path towards native reading. This is especially true if you take good advantage of the numerous opportunities throughout the day to reinforce your child's developing understanding of words.

These learning opportunities abound once you get in the habit of looking for them. For example, say you're on a stroller walk with your child and you come up to a stop sign. You should take a moment to point out and read the word "STOP" to your child. You only need to do this a few times to seed the process; soon your child will start singing out "Stop!" every time you come across another stop sign. Once this starts to happen—a simple "protoliterate" understanding that can develop very early with native reading—each succeeding time your child sees another stop sign, it will actually help your child's developing ability to read. This will even happen when children see signs while passively riding in the car and looking out the window. At first they may well be recognizing the sign primarily by its color and shape, but, with the foundation provided by letter play and the other native-reading techniques, they *will* notice the letters, too. Soon, they will naturally progress to truly reading the sign. And not long after this, they will become able to read and understand the word "stop" even out of the context of the roadside.

This sort of thing is why it's hard for me to quantify the amount of time per day I spent using native-reading techniques with my own children. It takes no extra time or particular effort to point out a few stop signs and to read them to your child, but with a foundation in native reading, this sort of activity becomes a powerful learning method. When you visit the zoo, for another example, certainly you should spend most of the time watching all the different animals. But instead of just saying the name of each animal you see, take the extra second or two to also point at the words in the signs by each exhibit, and read aloud the name of the animals while you do so. Just by consistently doing this little thing, you transform a trip to the zoo into wonderful native-reading practice. When grocery shopping, let your child hold the shopping list while riding in the grocery cart. Take a moment to point out each item on the list when you find it in the aisles. Grocery shopping is transformed into a native-reading treasure hunt.

Words are nearly everywhere in the modern world, so there are opportunities to utilize native-reading techniques nearly everywhere, too. And, to be honest, it soon becomes quite easy for a parent to do this because, very quickly, your native-reading child will begin to take the initiative.

"Mama, what's that sign say?"

"Why does the bulldozer say 'Cat' on it, Papa?"

As your child really starts to see the connection between written words and speech, the process rapidly snowballs.

Therefore, very soon, even on those days when you're particularly harried and can't even manage to read aloud during shopping, your child's curiosity will take over. While sitting quietly in the cart, independently your child will be looking around, noticing familiar words everywhere, recognizing these same words on the list, remembering the way you pronounced them last time. You and the native-reading techniques catalyze the process, but your child's natural intelligence and curiosity quickly make the process self-sustaining. Given that the world today is a hyperliterate place, it becomes almost impossible *not* to practice reading, once you get a good start on the process. Our world just makes so much more sense when you can read. Just like learning to talk, when children are given a good start on the path towards native reading, and when they live in a sufficiently rich environment, they soon reach a point where there is really no stopping them.

Because it has become increasingly popular recently, I want to briefly address baby signing, and its relation with native reading. Neither I nor his mother had heard much about baby signing when our son was born, so we never introduced Otto to signing when he was young. However, during the five years before our second child was born, we observed some friends' good experiences signing with their young children. Because of this, we introduced signing with our daughter, Freya, at an early age. Like many parents who try signing, we were amazed at how quickly she learned to understand and use the signs for things like "more" and "milk" and "cat". Learning signing seemed incredibly intuitive. We would demonstrate a sign just a few times and she would often catch on immediately. She had a small repertoire of baby signs before she was a year old. Signing allowed Freya to effectively communicate wants and needs, and also to simply share observations she made about the world (like when she saw a cat in real life or in a book); and it allowed her to do this before her vocal abilities were sufficiently developed to allow for speech. She was very enthusiastic about signing because it was such an effective way for her to communicate. I've known several other parents who have had similarly good experiences baby signing with their children. Signing also introduces children to their first "foreign language" at an early age—a language that parallels and corresponds to the spoken language that they hear from birth (and even before birth!). In this way I believe that signing children begin to appreciate correlations between different forms of language, which is a deep understanding they can extend to the written word, too. For these reasons, I believe that baby signing can be a great complement to native reading. By introducing visual symbols that stand for spoken words, signs provide a bridge to the more abstract written words that also stand for spoken words. So, by all means, if you want to sign, incorporate it into your play with your child.

If you choose to use baby signing you should, of course, adapt the native-reading techniques to make use of this new mode of communication. As a simple example, native-reading Technique 6, "Point, *consistently*, from the word for a thing to a picture of a thing, while saying that same word" can become, using signing, "Point, *consistently*, from the word for a thing to the *sign* for a thing, while saying that same word". Because many children find signing so intuitive there may be no need to actually point to the sign: just make the sign and point to the word the sign signifies. Technique 6 then becomes: "Point, *consistently*, to the word for a thing *as you make the sign for that thing*, while saying that same word". You get the idea. Done consistently, this makes the correlations between the written, signed, and spoken language intuitively clear for a child.

Of course, teaching native reading when using sign language is fundamentally the same as teaching it when only using spoken language. Just as when you correlate spoken words to written words, when you point from signs to written words you are not expecting your child to "get it" after the first few efforts. Rather, as always, the goal is to create a consistently correlated environment where children will discover the meaning of written words *on their own*, when they are ready. This is worth repeating because signing can be so easily intuitive for a child—children can so rapidly master at least a few favorite signs at a very early age—that this might lead you to expect your child to read with the same almost immediate results. Reading is a bit more abstract and complex than signing, and it will generally require more patience on the part of the parent.

For my daughter signing was a relatively brief stage of development, and she never developed a terribly large signing vocabulary. In fact, once her spoken vocabulary began to really take off, just after her first birthday, her spoken words began to gradually replace her signing vocabulary. A few of her favorite signs persisted longer ("milk" and "more" especially; in fact, for quite a while Freya would "talk in her sleep", as it were, by signing "milk" when she stirred during naps). But, despite being a brief stage, baby signing was a wonderful tool for communication. Signing allowed my daughter to know, from a very early age, that there was more than one way to communicate.

Finally, you may have noticed that none of the techniques of native reading involve any electronic device, computer game, video, or other high-tech method. Actually, I believe you should be very wary of any device or method that claims to help your child learn to read without *your* interaction. In general, young children naturally and appropriately prefer their parents' active involvement to any sort of electronic babysitter. It's not just that you're a better teacher, but, more fundamentally, it's that your children use your interest and enthusiasm to determine what is important in their world. Because of this, any "baby-genius" interactive device or impressive-looking video series is likely to be easily surpassed, in both enjoyment and effectiveness, by a mother reading a good book to her child, or by a father spelling silly rhyming words with bathtub letters. This does not mean that children won't eventually expand their reading ability by playing computer games, or by watching their favorite videos. They almost certainly will, if those things are to be found in your house. In fact, judiciously using these sorts of activities can later provide a fun and useful supplement (and, let's be honest, they also provide an occasional much-needed break for you). But they will never make up the core techniques of native reading. It is *your* interest and enthusiasm, your creativity and goofiness, along with your consistency, persistence, and patience that will make the techniques of native reading work—that, and your child's natural genius for learning languages, properly extended to the written word.

FIVE

Early Signs of Success,
Seeing Your Child's Progress

As I have emphasized throughout this book, when children are raised as native readers, there *is* a level of patience that is required by parents. This is quite in contrast to the children's point of view, where the correlative techniques of native reading simply become part of their normal play. Promoting native reading involves, by design, very little traditional direct instruction. The parents of native readers are put in the position of patiently waiting for their child to make palpable progress. As parents, you create the richly correlative environment, and then your child takes it from there, cognitively speaking. Children make the connections between spoken and written language—which the correlative techniques of native reading are designed to make intuitive—and they do this on their own initiative and at their own pace.

Patience, even faith, is especially needed during your child's first year. In a child's first year of life the native-reading techniques establish very important neurological groundwork for deep and early literacy, but obvious signs of progress can be hard to discern at first. After all, at this age babies are only just learning to crawl and walk, and by the end of their first year they usually have, at most, just a few words in their vocabulary. Children *are* learning at an astounding rate during their first twelve to eighteen months, but at times it can be very hard to tell exactly *what* they're learning—often you're just glad they're no longer spitting up on you! This chapter is to help parents catch sight of their children's subtle but unambiguous signs of early progress towards native reading. In this chapter I detail some early behavioral milestones that are likely to occur well before children actually start reading, but which clearly indicate that they are firmly *on the path* to native reading.

I do believe that if you use the native-reading techniques detailed in the previous chapter, your child's overall progress will likely be much faster than you ever expected (not to mention what most of your friends and relatives expect, if they're not yet familiar with native reading!). But there *will* be days when it seems like your child is making no obvious headway. Be assured that this is exactly as it should be. The process of learning to read natively, like learning to talk, is inherently nonlinear. There will be times when decisive thresholds of understanding are reached. These can be followed by exhilarating periods of amazingly rapid progress. But these will be interspersed with periods of time that represent plateaus of understanding, where little change may be apparent for a while. (I do believe, however, that a plateau period actually often represents a very important time where the neural organization and consolidation of understanding is taking place—consolidation that is critical to further progress but which may not be obvious in external behavior.)

Some parents may even find themselves wishing for some highly formulaic material for their child to complete—workbooks, exercise sheets, or the like—to provide some palpable proof of progress in the form of an increasing stack of "work" completed. Although I can sympathize with a parent's desire for such a system, I believe this would be counterproductive. Children do not learn to speak in such a systematic way, and they will not best learn to read natively in such an artificial environment either. Again, remember that you don't really teach native reading, you just foster it; *you* create the richly-correlated native-reading environment, and then wait for your child to make the connections. You can encourage this process, but it cannot be forced. So teaching native reading (like much of parenthood) does require a kind of faith by the parents, although, if you understand the theory behind the method, it can be an entirely rational variety of faith.

Fortunately, there are a number of sometimes subtle, but actually very important, signposts of success along the way to native reading. These signposts can help you keep that necessary faith in the process. As your child's general comprehension of language progresses, and as the native-reading techniques increase your child's understanding of the technology of the written word, there are small changes in behavior that actually indicate *enormous* progress on the path towards early and deep literacy. Recognizing these signs of success is gratifying for parents who are working to foster a native-reading environment for their child. Recognizing these signs of success is also important because it allows you to take your child's new skills into account as you organize subsequent play and learning. As milestones in understanding are reached, new emphasis in particular types of play becomes appropriate.

I have already indicated some of these signs of success when I detailed the specific techniques of native reading in the last chapter, but providing specific examples here will make you more prepared to help your child learn to read. It also gives you an overview of the early arc of progress expected in a child learning to read natively.

Sign of Success 1: Tag gazing

In a child's first year it can be hard to see obvious benefits from the techniques of native reading. In the first months of life the visual system is still organizing and maturing, so reading and text pointing to your four-month-old may sometimes feel slightly silly. But starting consistent reading early is very important. It's fine if, at the outset, your reading amounts to only five minutes each day with just a short book or two. You can start reading as soon as your child has the head control and steadiness of gaze to allow it. By being read to from early infancy, your child will become accustomed to taking an interest in books, which is wonderful in itself. But reading to a child this early does something even more important precisely *because* your child's visual system is still developing during these early months. By reading and by engaging in letter play and other native-reading activities in this period, a child will actually learn to *see* letters and text more natively. In addition to a child's strong innate "search images" for faces and for bold patterns, and to children's later learned search images for animals and their favorite toys, a native reader will also develop deep search images for writing, both for individual letters and for text. Because of this, native readers have a greater interest in the text in their environment, and this starts from a very early age. This early interest can lead to a simple but profound milestone that both of my children reached before nine months: tag gazing. That is, babies raised as native readers will often develop a particular interest in the nearly ubiquitous tags which are found on all their stuffed animals, on many other toys, on clothes, and on other "baby gear", too. Their interest in tags will not be, by any means, at the expense of their typical interest in the more usual aspects of their toys. Like most babies, native readers will play with, hug, chew on, knock over, and toss about their assortment of stuffed animals. But in addition to their interest in the faces and ears and fuzzy fur of their toys, they will also take special notice of the tags.

To be sure, many children take *some* notice of tags, but there is a sure sign that a native reader's interest in tags is primarily an interest in the text. In contrast to the way children, native reader or not, look at a teddy bear's nose, or eyes—and in contrast to the way non-native-reading babies typically look at tags, when they do—native-reading children will often look *very* closely at the tags, and they may even make obvious attempts to look at the text in the right orientation. My son was a champion tag gazer, and at times he would actually rotate his whole body in an arc about the toy, rather than rotating the toy, while keeping his eyes a few inches from the tiny text of the tag. When Otto had scooted around sufficiently, so that the writing on the tag was finally right side up, he would often noticeably pause for moment, satisfied, and then move on to another tag. While doing this he also typically made a funny little grunting sound of deep concentration, a sound similar to the noise I've heard other concentrating children make when playing with foam puzzles, or peg boards, or similar challenging toys. The very *close* inspection of tags is simply an attempt to see the tiny text on a tag at an apparent size close to the apparent magnitude of the writing children usually see: the large text of their favorite children's books. When peering close at a tag, native-reading babies are trying to match the size of what they are seeing with the size of their search image for text; they are trying to make the mapping as close a match as possible.

Otto's tag gazing was so striking that a relative bought him a baby toy that consisted of a squishy ball covered all over with dozens of tags of various colors. Though it seemed the perfect gift, as it turned out, after the first few inspections, he actually had very little interest in it. The reason was very simple: with the exception of one "real" tag, every other tag on this toy was just a colored flap with no writing or text of any sort! Because of the lack of text, I think Otto found it fairly uninteresting, even disappointing, to the point that he would reject this superficially magnificent-looking toy, and instead would choose to peer at the little tags (with text!) on his new pair of booties.

Sign of Success 2: A preference for viewing text right side up

It may already be apparent in native readers' first tag gazing, but even when it is not obvious quite that early, if you observe native-reading children carefully, they will show an early preference for viewing text in its proper orientation. That is, they will clearly prefer text right side up. After only a few months of consistent letter and word play, of reading with text pointing, and other early techniques, if you watch carefully you will notice that at times native-reading children are not placing their play letters completely randomly. More often than not, they will place them right side up. Soon after they are first able to pick up and manipulate a book, native-reading children will tend to hold it in the proper orientation, even when the pages they are looking at have no pictures, only text. As with tag gazing, if, say, native-reading toddlers see some junk mail with large bold writing on it which has fallen on the floor, often they will move themselves around, rotating their point of view, until they are viewing the text right side up.

If you are not on the lookout for this behavior, it can be quite subtle, because the "righting" of text is done naturally and even "thoughtlessly" most of the time. It's not that native-reading one-year-olds have a clear, explicit realization, "Hey, this is wrong," when they see upside down writing. But they *will* go somewhat out of their way to view writing in the way that feels most right to them. Because of their early and consistent exposure to the written word, native-reading children have a search image for writing that right side up text best satisfies, so they will prefer this.

This preference by itself certainly does not mean that they're reading yet. But it does mean they have started on the path towards reading. They already behave with the written word in a way that is sensible, rather than random. This preference is not a mere parlor trick, rather, by holding their point of view constant, their orientation preference greatly simplifies all subsequent learning about words. Without the simple notion that there *is* a right way up for writing (and, as a consequence, a wrong way up, too), the differences between a "b" and a "d", and a "q" and a "p" are actually quite surprising. (The importance of this and related issues are discussed more fully in Chapter 7, "Can Native Reading Prevent Dyslexia?")

Of course, even children well on their way to native reading will not display a preference for proper text orientation in all of their play. When toddlers are having fun throwing their foam letters about the living room—being the little masters of chaos that they are—they probably won't care in which orientation they pick up the letters. Or if they're playing peekaboo behind one of their books, not looking at the book at all but, rather, simply using it as a hiding place, then that book may as well be upside down, sideways, or diagonal for that matter. As I discussed in Chapter 4, it is also common for children to occasionally experiment by doing things precisely *wrong* for a time. For a spell they may view writing not randomly, but *only* upside down, or they might experiment by viewing it every way possible *except* right side up. Don't worry that children are "learning it wrong" when this sort of thing happens; and, in general, I don't think you should try to correct them when they do this, either. Let children experiment; the truth is, a brief fascination with doing things wrong is generally a sure sign that they already have a clear conception of the way things *should* be done.

Sign of Success 3: Learning the names of letters

Because of their early exposure to letters and words, and particularly because of consistent naming and manipulation of the alphabet during letter play, children raised to read natively do not see letters as most children do. For most children letters are meaningless abstract objects. But for native-reading children, letters are a meaningful part of the world, and letters and words are things that pique their curiosity. In fact, long before they can read, and even before they know the sounds that each letter makes, native-reading children are likely to learn the names of the letters of the alphabet. Because this can happen quite early, children may know all the letter names well before they can accurately *pronounce* every name. But they will begin to reliably recognize at least some of the letters very early in toddlerdom. For example, when you ask for, say, a "B" while assembling a word with them, you will soon find that they can reliably find it for you.

While simple letter recognition is certainly very far from true reading, its early appearance clearly shows that the native-reading techniques are helping a child to see and distinguish the fundamental units of written language. A child who knows the names of even only a few letters has already taken the important step of correctly judging that the symbols of writing are an important part of his or her world. Taking this letter-naming step early, and gaining familiarity and search images for text even earlier, makes learning to read *much* more intuitive during a child's subsequent development. For native-reading children the alphabet is *not* "all Greek to me" anymore.

As always, you should not worry if, after the first appearance of letter recognition, your child seems sometimes uninterested or is inaccurate when naming letters. The important step is that a child can recognize *any* letters at all, and that a child *sometimes* expresses an interest in text. It's really not very important that children do this particularly often or accurately. In fact, when children recognize their first few letters, while you should certainly encourage whatever interest they have, you should resist the urge to *press* them to learn the entire alphabet right away. Just as you were thrilled with your child's first spoken words, and probably did not respond to this milestone by immediately drilling your child to learn ten more, you should let children set the pace when they are learning their letters. Also, you shouldn't warp the naturalness of their play in an attempt to test the extent of their new ability. The gentler methods of text pointing, letter play, word assembly, and the other native-reading techniques are a more natural way to consolidate a child's understanding.

There is an important principle behind the fact that parents should not be surprised if, after first displaying an ability to recognize a letter, their child goes on to make many mistakes. The principle to remember is this: there *is* such a thing as an *intelligent mistake*. This is particularly the case for mistakes of overgeneralization, which are often *very* intelligent mistakes, although they are frequently interpreted otherwise. Here's the sort of thing I mean: while assembling a word, you might find yourself saying out loud, really just to yourself, "Where's that 'D'?" Then you find yourself amazed to see your child, for the very first time, dig deep into a pile of play letters and hold out the "D" for you. Children will often first make a breakthrough like this as if it were nothing at all, as if they had always helped you like this. This is likely to happen long before you expected it—after all, your child may not even be talking yet! Or, if reading this book convinces you that your child is capable of things like letter recognition at an early age, still, you will almost certainly not be expecting it when it actually first happens. So what will you do when it does happen? You will probably get very excited and direct *heaps* of praise and attention on your child. You might well call your spouse at work, and perhaps your mother in Florida, too. She will probably insist that her grandbaby is a categorical *genius*. All this activity and excitement will make a huge impression on your child. After the phone calls are finished and the excitement dies down, you probably won't be able to resist a little test: you ask for the "D" again, probably directly this time. Your own eyes will be wide with anticipation as your child immediately plunges *both* hands into the pile of letters and, with the brightest of smiles, confidently presents you with a *"Q" and a "K"*. Disappointment floods over you. Your child is not a genius; it was all just a fluke. Do you call your mother back and break the bad news?

Don't call her back. Just think back and realize that when your child retrieved the "D" correctly, he or she did two things that are *very* unlikely to have occurred by chance. First, they recognized that by "D" you meant a letter at all, *any* letter, but not another sort of object: this is a huge realization in itself. Second, they picked the *correct* letter out of the pile. It was almost certainly not a fluke. You see, for a child used to native-reading methods, finding the "D" probably just felt natural and quite effortless. It's not that your child really thought particularly hard and then explicitly *decided* that "D" was the right letter. In fact, if you told your child, after the disappointing second try, that the "Q" and "K" were the "wrong" letters, they'd probably have no idea what you were talking about. At this preverbal stage their successful first try was probably more accurately described by saying that they just had a *sense* that you were looking for one of the letters, and when they rummaged about through their pile of letters, the "D" was the one they *felt* you wanted. It felt right to pick it up, rather like it feels right to children to echo back early babytalk to their parents. But after children do such a thing successfully, without much consideration at all, it is their parents' sudden excitement and attention that makes the big impression. If they are tested soon after such a breakthrough, what children want is a repeat performance from you: the excitement, the attention, the wide eyes. The subtle feeling that led them to find the *correct* letter has probably been quite eclipsed. When asked to find the "D" again, they are in a hurry to please you and to start the excitement all over again. In fact, instead of the "Q" and "K", they might just as well have presented you with a stuffed animal or an empty sippy cup if that were closer at hand! This is natural. So you shouldn't be disappointed, and you shouldn't discourage your child when they do it wrong after first doing it right. Soon enough, after making a breakthrough like this, a child's ability *will* become accurate and reliable; and it will happen sooner if you don't distract them with too much explicit criticism *or* praise.

Even when children have learned to recognize many letters, you should also expect them to make mistakes like confusing "d" and "b", "M" and "N", or "D" and "O". Such "dyslexic-like" mistakes are a normal phase. It would actually be strange if children *didn't* make these sorts of mistakes before they had time to master the more subtle distinctions of our visually-confusing alphabet. I certainly think it is misguided to worry that your child might be dyslexic after a few such mistakes. (In fact, not only do I believe that you shouldn't worry if your two-year-old makes some "dyslexic" mistakes, but, as discussed in Chapter 7, I think a child who deals with this *early on*, a child who learns the quirks of the written word *natively*, along with learning speech, may actually *avoid* the root cause of many dyslexias.)

So the important aspect of learning letter names at a young age is not how accurate the skill is, or how often it is displayed. The important point is it indicates that your child is already developing the foundations for deep literacy. Learning letter names indicates that the otherwise abstract and nonintuitive symbols of the written word have been transformed into normal and *meaningful* objects in your child's world. This early cognitive breakthrough sets the stage for the learning that's soon to come.

Sign of Success 4: Miming and "playing at" reading

Because reading is a normal part of life in their home, and because they already have an interest in, and some understanding of, the written word, children raised as native readers are likely to mime or play at reading from an early age. My daughter, for example, loved to arrange her multitude of stuffed animals carefully in bed, give them goodnight kisses, and then "read" each of them a book. She began doing this when she was barely talking. At this age the "reading" was mostly a cursory opening and closing of the book, during which she might say a remembered or improvised word or two. Then she typically concluded with a firm, "The End," before saying goodnight to each tucked-in animal. Later, when she was two-and-a-half and three years of age, Freya still enjoyed tucking her animals and dolls into bed like this. At this age, however, she would read entire books to them. What had started as play had transformed from pantomime into effective and independent reading practice. The game became a powerful and fun way she could continue to improve her reading, even when her parents were otherwise occupied. Both of my children were so used to text pointing that, when they played at reading, they typically pointed at the text themselves. Already, they were raising their own teddy bears and raggedy anns to be native readers, too!

Play reading can start very early. Soon after he could sit up, at around six months of age, my son enjoyed working through a stack of baby books. He would pick each one up for a moment, babble a bit while flipping a page or two, and then he would toss the book aside and reach for the next book in the stack.

Miming and playing at reading is a long way from true literacy, but it already indicates a child's interest and enthusiasm for books. Play is fun, but it is also a seriously effective way of learning. When children enjoy "playing at" reading at a young age like this, it is another early sign that they are on the path towards native reading. Such children already have a repertoire of social habits and games that allow later practice and progress in reading to develop perfectly naturally.

Sign of Success 5: Recognizing a few favorite written words

Probably the most striking early sign of success is that native-reading children are likely to begin recognizing a small number of favorite and familiar written words when they are still very young—sometimes even before they're a year old. These first words are generally words that they see often, words that represent things they especially like, and words that they encounter in stereotyped contexts during their native-reading play.

For my own children this early word recognition started just before the age of one year for my son, and at about one-and-a-half for my daughter. Among their early words were their own names, "Mama" and "Papa", and the names of many of their favorite animals, "Cat", "Dog", "Cow", "Pig" and so on. Very common words, especially words like "then", "but" and "and", which often start a new page in children's books, were also among the words they learned very early. Otto and Freya also began recognizing simple combinations of words, too; identifying, for example, "The End" at the conclusion of a book.

Such word recognition can happen so early that you may have to rein in your expectations a bit. Your child is not yet truly reading. In fact, it may be some months or even a year after the first word recognition before children are truly reading independently. The first word recognition comes because children are using shortcuts, memory, and context to recognize their favorite words. It is not yet a general ability to comprehend written language. Children at this stage can therefore be fairly easily "fooled"; for example, if you were to give them a book with a last page that said "That's it", children at this stage are likely to "read" it confidently as, "The End." But this does not mean that such an early ability to recognize words is not important. These first words act as prototypes for a child. For example, every time native-reading children see the words "The End" and recognize them, whether they hear the words in their mind or actually say them out loud, they powerfully reinforce the semantic correlation between the spoken and written words and the phonetic correlation between the letters and the sounds of the words.

So while the shortcuts, the contextual clues, and the other methods children use in early word recognition do distinguish it from true reading, these methods are *not* "cheating" in any way. They are intelligent techniques for making sense of writing and should be encouraged. These same methods will help them later as their ability to understand writing naturally expands and generalizes. For example, well before her second birthday, my daughter recognized her name reliably when I would assemble it with letters. But at first she also made many "false positive" mistakes, too: when I would assemble any word of about the same length as her name which also started with an "F", she would read it as her own name, "Freya". So, she certainly wasn't yet reading at 18 months. But the shortcuts she was using—looking at the first letter and the overall gestalt of the word to decide what it was—are *part* of the cognitive repertoire that even fully-fluent readers use. Also, she clearly associated the written word (even when she was wrong) with her own spoken name, and this in itself is a very important intellectual step on the path to reading. And "F" did, in fact, became one of the first letters she reliably recognized. It was also one of the first letters for which she reliably associated the correct sound: even when stumped by a word that started with an "F", she would generally make an "f" sound as she thought about it (although, as for many toddlers and preschoolers, for some time her "f"s sounded pretty much like breathy "p"s).

So don't mistake it for true reading, but do encourage and enjoy your child's first ability to recognize words. It is an additional sign that your child is solidly on the path to native reading.

T he five milestones detailed here are likely early signs of progress towards native reading. Later—but not much later—the signs of success become patently obvious. For example, when your two or three-year-old starts shocking the cashiers at the grocery store by spontaneously reading their nametags, well, you won't need any guidance then to see your child's success at reading. But during the first year or two, keeping these signposts in mind can certainly help.

I believe most native-reading children will show evidence of these milestone behaviors. However, I suspect that some perfectly normal children will not exhibit *all* of these milestones—including children who are, indeed, solidly on the path towards native reading. Every child is different, both in the timing and the course of their cognitive development. I would not be surprised if some babies never took particular notice of tags, for example. With my son, tag gazing was very conspicuous. But in comparison, my daughter's early interest in tags was much less obvious. Sometimes these behavioral signposts, even if present, may be so subtle or brief that they may entirely escape a parent's notice. Because of this natural variability, this listing of early milestones is *not* meant to be a *necessary* list. It is not a list to be checked off as your child passes each stage. And you certainly should not worry needlessly if you don't see evidence of one or another of these behaviors in your own child. If you raise your children in a sufficiently-correlated native-reading home, soon enough you should see completely obvious and undeniable signs of their growing understanding of the written word. Just remember that each child will follow the particular developmental path which is most natural for him or her.

S I X

Some Common Misconceptions
About Native Reading

When you are the parent of a native reader, you will find that most people are absolutely delighted, even thrilled, when they see a two-year-old child reading. However, there are also a few people who are *not* pleased when they see such a thing. Sometimes this is the result of simple misunderstanding, or a lack of information, but negative reactions can also result from outright resistance to the idea that reading can or should start at so young an age. I believe there are three primary motivations for such resistance to native reading:

(1) The first is the understandable, if not exactly commendable, competitiveness of some parents. Such parents can have a negative reaction when they see a native-reading child, particularly when the native reader is considerably younger, yet a much more advanced reader, than their own child. In the (thankfully rare) worst of these parents, there can be knee-jerk responses that typically go one of two ways: sometimes competitive parents are quick to berate the intelligence of their own child (even going so far as directly insulting their child in his or her presence!), other times they immediately posit some spurious, generally not at all well thought out, downside to reading so young.

(2) The second motivation that can prompt resistance to native reading is the feeling of many people that reading is a difficult and necessarily "older" activity which young children either cannot, or somehow should not, master. I believe that this notion is to some extent a cultural relic of the fact that widespread literacy of *adults* is actually quite a recent phenomenon, common only in the last few generations—and adult literacy is not, in fact, yet universal, even in wealthy nations. There is often more than a bit of psychological insecurity involved in this motivation, too; some adults can find it quite challenging to their sense of the proper age and skill hierarchy when they see a two-year-old fluently read "May help lower your cholesterol," off the back of a cereal box. This can be especially challenging for adults who themselves cannot easily read a word like "cholesterol".

(3) Finally, there is another understandable but unfortunate source of resistance to native reading that I've encountered in a few members of the teaching profession. For example, at the first preschool my son attended there was one teacher who went out of her way to tell me, apropos of nothing, really, "We have *no time* here to help a *two-year-old* read!" This was an especially gratuitous comment because by this point Otto did not, in fact, need any help at all in reading (he was actually nearing his third birthday and was a fully-fluent reader). I think that, in addition to having their own versions of the first two motivations for resistance, some teachers also harbor a few teacher-specific motivations that can lead them to resist native reading. First, they believe that having a two-year-old who can read may portend more work for them, or at least work to which they are unaccustomed. They feel that they may need to change the way they do things in their classroom because their teaching materials and methods may be inappropriate for a child who is already fluently reading. Some teachers worry that

they might be expected to actually sit and read a book to such a child on occasion, and this is a prospect that not every preschool teacher views with pleasure. Put bluntly, I believe that some teachers resist the idea of native reading because, to their narrow interest as they perceive it, a young reader represents extra effort and might necessitate unwelcome changes in their way of doing things (and, of course, for people who are very set in their ways, *any* change can be unwelcome). More admirably, many teachers find it very rewarding when *they* help teach a child to read, and these same teachers can, at first, find themselves feeling a little useless when they are confronted with a two-year-old who can already read very competently. (I've found that teachers who have this more laudable feeling can come around very quickly when they soon realize that native-reading children, despite their mastery of the mechanics of reading, are still, after all, just two and three-year-olds, and they therefore quite literally have a world yet to learn. Also, precisely *because* of their early mastery of reading, native readers tend to be very teachable, which is gratifying for a dedicated teacher, even if some of what you can teach a native reader may be more advanced than preschool teachers are typically used to.) By the way, we quickly found another preschool for our son, where his teachers were completely supportive of his early reading.

In addressing likely misconceptions and objections to native reading, my purpose is twofold. First, I hope it is useful for parents reading this book who might themselves feel a nagging resistance to native reading, and who might profit from seeing their objections articulated and directly answered. Second, I hope that parents who successfully raise native-reading children will find this chapter useful when they find themselves in the position of explaining their child's precocious reading ability to friends, family, and teachers. It can be handy to have a ready set of explanations for responding to people who, while often delighted, can sometimes be simply flabbergasted, and intensely curious, when they encounter a fluently-reading two-year-old.

Misconception #1: You have to be a genius to read before the age of three.

The truth is, you have to be a genius to learn to *talk* before the age of three. But, fortunately, nearly every child is just such a genius! Many parents have been amazed by the way their child can go from speaking only a few words at the age of one, and then, only a year or two later, this same child has somehow transformed into a seemingly non-stop and fully-fluent talker, prattling on about his or her fascinations of the moment. The reason native reading works is that it takes advantage of this natural genius for learning spoken language. By creating an environment sufficiently rich in consistent correlations between spoken language and written language, native reading simply *extends* a child's natural language ability into the realm of the written word.

So you do have to be a genius to read so young, but I don't believe you have to be an *unusual* genius. To be a native reader, you just need to be the sort of creative and curious genius that a two-year-old child already is.

However, I believe this misconception may be inspired by a valid, but misinterpreted observation. Specifically, I believe that the *converse* statement may be true. That is, while you don't need to be an unusual genius to read before three, I believe that being a native reader might make you more likely to *become* a genius. Because native readers gain language fluency earlier, more deeply, and in its written form—and because literacy is a fundamental tool for further intellectual growth—it's a fairly straightforward consequence that native reading will generally help a child *use* the skill of reading to learn many important and interesting things. And, like language itself, native readers will tend to learn these things, which reading makes accessible, earlier and more deeply, too.

You see, learning to read is *not* a glorified parlor trick: encouraging native reading is not at all like teaching your child to memorize all the state capitals, for example, which is a specialized and largely useless set of information which has little connection to more general and more important knowledge. Honestly, I don't know why anyone would want to clutter up a child's brain with such trivia. Reading, in contrast, is very different: reading is a fundamental skill that gives your child fluent access to nearly all the information of human culture. Reading is not an end in itself; it helps a child to develop his or her unique talents, intelligence, and interests. By reading earlier and more effortlessly, the process of further intellectual development can start earlier, and learning will be more rewarding and less frustrating for a child.

Therefore, I am not at all surprised by cases of famous and accomplished writers, moguls, mathematicians, and other "geniuses" who were, in fact, early readers. I think this observation is often the root of the misconception that you have to be a genius to read so young. In fact, when they first saw my young children read precociously, several different people have brought up the tale of Mozart reading and writing music at a very young age. My point is that while Mozart's genius might have, in part, led to his early musical literacy, it may also have been his early fluency reading and writing music that helped to *develop* his genius.

Misconception #2: Children aren't supposed to read before they are three.

Viewed from a certain perspective, reading *is* an unnatural act: it is a cultural innovation that has only become widespread in the last few generations. So, from that perspective, this misconception is not a misconception at all. But, remember, from this same perspective, reading is *still* an unnatural act for a child in kindergarten or in the first grade. Even adults aren't *supposed* to read. Until the last few hundred years, only a tiny minority of people on this planet could fluently read and write. (By the way, many other aspects of modern life are unnatural in the same sense that reading is unnatural: e.g., typing on a keyboard, driving a car, riding a bicycle, finding square roots, buying insurance, etc.)

But, in an important way, the belief that children aren't supposed to read before the age of three is a damaging misconception. Learning to read early makes sense because it *is* natural to learn to talk early in childhood. Talking is generally mastered between the ages of one and three (although the neural foundations of learning speech do start during the first months of life). The benefit of native reading is that it harnesses this natural developmental window, and uses it to learn the deeply-related skill of reading right along with talking. By doing this early, deep neural connections will be made between the naturally-acquired oral language and the deeply-related, but unnaturally abstract, act of reading. Doing this makes reading a less abstract and more natural skill. Reading becomes *natively known,* just as the ability to talk and to understand speech is known natively. A native reader has a "mother tongue" not only in the spoken language, but also, deeply, in the written language.

While I think the optimum time to learn to *read* is from one to three years, I want to reiterate what I've mentioned elsewhere in this book: I do not believe children should be expected to *write* until considerably later—at least not conventionally, with a pencil or pen on paper. With my children, and especially for my son, the fine motor skills that made it possible to learn writing without frustration came a few years later than reading. For native readers, the cognitive skill of reading becomes somewhat decoupled from the physical skill of writing. Very large format writing is certainly possible: say, with a paintbrush on paper, chalk on a sidewalk, or with a stick on wet sand at the beach. In fact, for a native-reading child this is likely to be a delight and I think it's great for parents to encourage this sort of play. But don't expect a two-year-old child to sit at a desk and neatly draw letters within the confines of the dotted lines—no matter how fluently that same two-year-old can read. The usual format of worksheets used in kindergartens is simply too small for toddlers. Their fine motor skills need a few more years to develop. Some ability typing is actually likely to come earlier, if it's encouraged. Of course, native-reading children are able to assemble words from fully formed letters as soon as they begin reading, for example by using magnetic letters on the refrigerator. They are also likely to enjoy "dictating" letters, lists, and stories, while an adult or older sibling writes it out for them. With this sort of help, a child's written creative production can come early, but real facility with longhand writing generally takes a few more years to arrive.

Misconception #3: If most children actually have the ability to read before the age of three, why do only very, very few children read that early now?

I believe the reason most children, at present, do not learn to read at the optimal age of one to three years is very simple: currently very few children are raised in an environment that sufficiently helps them to do this. It is a question of a child's environment, not of a child's ability. The typical early environment of a child does not adequately introduce the symbols of written language, and it does not do this in the engagingly interactive way that is appropriate for this age. Also, the correlation of written and spoken language is not made clearly and consistently apparent to children. So, at present, a child's natural and effortless ability to learn spoken language before three is only rarely extended into the written word. I believe this represents a wasted opportunity—not only a wasted opportunity to read earlier, but, at least for some children, a wasted opportunity to read more easily and fluently, and with better comprehension, throughout their life.

Recognizing that the nonintuitive, abstract letters which make up our written language are *meaningful* does not happen easily for young children in most home and preschool environments today. I think this recognition is one of the most important "rate-limiting" steps towards the early acquisition of reading. It is not for nothing that most children's books are primarily picture books; seeing that nonabstract *pictures* are meaningful comes naturally for most children, but seeing that abstract *text* is meaningful requires the structured, correlative environment that the techniques of native reading are designed to provide. In such a native-reading environment, however, I don't believe that recognizing text as meaningful is particularly hard for most children. Fundamentally, learning to read is not harder than learning to talk, it's just less intuitive. The native-reading techniques help create an environment where learning to read *is* intuitive, and where becoming literate is as natural as learning to talk.

Creating a native-reading environment does take some effort by parents and caregivers. However, it turns out that the majority of this effort involves only subtle, but consistent, modification of common parenting habits: for example, playing games, singing songs, and reading to your child. Growing up in a native-reading home doesn't require notable extra effort for a child. By this I don't mean to say that learning language is *easy*—in fact, computer scientists would be considered geniuses if their programs could acquire natural spoken language just half as successfully as the average child!—but what I am saying is that reading, given the proper environment, becomes a complex task that children nevertheless pick up with almost miraculous ease. And children learn to read natively like this with *joy*, in much the same way children learn to talk, or walk, or in the way that birds learn to fly.

Misconception #4: It's not right to push children to learn to read so young.

If you taught babies and toddlers to read the way older children are typically taught in school, I would have this objection myself. But that's not how the method of native reading works. In fact, in a very real way you cannot *teach* native reading at all at this age, you can only *promote* it. But properly promoted, very young children can pick up reading on their own initiative, at their own pace, and when they are each individually ready for it. There are no worksheets or drills or exams in native reading. It is not a grind. Instead, native reading works by setting up obvious *correlations* between spoken and written language; it is then your child's natural genius for language that picks up on these correlations. Done with consistency and patience, this leads *naturally* to reading. You cannot, and you should not, push children or somehow force them in any way. In fact, I believe that any attempt to force this process will generally only distract a young child, and will greatly slow down progress towards reading.

My children both learned to read essentially independently. They learned in much the same way that they learned to crawl and walk and, particularly, in the same way that they, like nearly all other children, learned to talk. By independently I don't mean that they learned to read *alone*; what I mean is that they learned at their own pace and through play that they very much enjoyed. To be honest, my children enjoyed native-reading play so much that they sometimes had more stamina for reading play than their parents did! In truth, with native reading, it's the *parent* who may feel a bit pushed, on occasion, rather than the children. When children begin to really discover reading, their enthusiasm can be prodigious. Their tireless energy and attention span for reading can sometimes be intellectually exhausting. It may remind you of the way newly-mobile children can make your back positively *ache* during the first weeks after they learn to walk: the stage where you follow toddlers around, a step or two behind, hunched over and ready to catch them, as they tirelessly zigzag among all the new obstacles, dangers, and delights which their new skill opens up to them. Just as a baby's first steps cannot usefully be forced by parents, when reading is learned natively it is learned at a child's own initiative and a child's own pace. And reading progress is fostered through interactive *play* with their parents. The native-reading techniques help you create a rich, interesting, and fun environment in which your child is encouraged to spontaneously discover reading, and to find joy in doing so. Your child will learn to read by observation, by interaction and, essentially, by *playing*.

Teaching native reading means simply extending your child's spontaneous genius for language into the written word. Nobody worries about pushing a child into talking too early. Taught natively, you cannot read too early either. The techniques of native reading help you create a home where children learn to read using the same language aptitude that naturally leads them to speak—an aptitude that is burgeoning in children between the ages of one and three.

Misconception #5: There are some rare children who have learned to read very early without the methods of this book.

This is not really a misconception at all, in fact, it is absolutely true. The misconception here is to suppose that I'm claiming otherwise. It is true that very early readers occasionally pop up here and there throughout recorded history. I believe there are two primary reasons for this:

(1) A few children are lucky enough to have had parents, or other caregivers, who intuitively created an environment that successfully promoted native reading. Actually, I believe that native readers are probably becoming somewhat less rare these days as more people heed recent recommendations to read to their children from an early age. However, I do not believe that current practices are *likely* to lead to native reading—not even the best practices of very supportive parents who read to their children every day from birth. In contrast, if the simple methods of this book are put into practice, I think it will be common to find fluently-reading two and three-year-olds.

(2) As in every other ability, there is a great deal of individual variation in how easily children are able to master reading, and in when they are most ready to do it. A child who has abundant curiosity about abstract things, and who has an attention span to match, may well pick up reading at the age of three in an environment only moderately rich in correlations between written and spoken language; simply being in a literate, educated home with dedicated parents may be sufficient for such a child. But most children, with different strengths, will not make the connections necessary to become an early reader in even this supportive environment.

In contrast, the native-reading techniques are intentionally based on the natural abilities that essentially all children share. The different strengths and personalities of each child will certainly lead to different individual pathways to reading, but the end result should generally be the same: a deep and fluent understanding of the written word at what most people consider a strikingly early age.

My experience with my own two children shows the truth of this. My son, Otto, always had a particular interest in signs and symbols from an early age. For example, as soon as he could grasp objects, he loved to play with his multicolored bathtub letters. Otto knew all the letters of the alphabet soon after his first birthday, and he delighted in this knowledge. He starting reading at eighteen months, and for most of his childhood, he read with just about the same level of fluency with which he could speak. Otto quickly progressed until, by the age of two, he was fluent enough to read long chapter books. By the age of three he was already a considerably better speller than I am (and I'm not *that* bad), completely unflustered by silent letters, hard versus soft "c"s, "ie"s and "ei"s, and other such difficulties.

In contrast, my second-born child, Freya, was comparatively uninterested in letters and words through her first two-and-a-half years. She was, perhaps more typically, focused on the pictures in books and generally ignored the text. However, I continued to use my correlational methods with her because the logic behind them was so compelling to me. So, for example, even though she generally seemed to be ignoring my consistent text pointing when I read books to her, I continued to do it. I was in the habit by this time, after the experience with my son. But I never tried to *make* Freya look at the words. I simply persisted in my techniques, reasoning that she would take notice when she was ready. Freya, by the way, was always such a "stubborn" or, I like to think, "opinionated" child, that somehow *pushing* her to read, or pushing her to do just about anything else she wasn't enthusiastic about, was seldom a viable option. The moment she felt she was being pushed into *anything* was the moment she usually determined she was going to have nothing of it! Then, at around two-and-a-half years, Freya, too, suddenly starting asking me (or more accurately, *commanding* me) to point to the words—"Point, Papa. Point!"—on those occasions when I was being momentarily forgetful or lazy and was not already text pointing. The way this happened, quite out of the blue, makes me quite sure that she had actually been taking notice of the words for a long time, at least subconsciously. Within a month or two she was reading individual words on her own and very quickly, before her third birthday, she too was reading fluently. I suspect that Freya's very nonlinear learning trajectory will prove more typical for native reading acquisition; only the experience of many more families will tell for sure.

Misconception #6: My child didn't learn to read until six years old and yet is now a very fluent reader, therefore the theory of native reading must be wrong.

There certainly are some children who learn to read relatively late and who, yet, eventually become very fluent readers. What does native reading have to say about this? Does this observation contradict the foundations of native reading? I don't believe so. In fact, I myself didn't read particularly early, but I consider myself a pretty good reader now. I'm not a terribly fast reader, it's true, but soon after I began to read in school I generally read with good comprehension and fluency.

I don't believe that native reading is the only way to become a good reader, but I do believe that it is generally a better, easier, and more reliable way to become a good reader. I think native reading will allow a greater proportion of children to become very good readers; and, for some children, it may prevent a life-long struggle with the written word.

Just as there exist rare people who have such an unusual aptitude for foreign languages (and who retain sufficient neural flexibility later in life) that they can quite easily learn a second language as late as early adulthood, there is certainly a great deal of natural variation in aptitude for reading, too. Many children apparently do fine with current practices: they learn to read, with only a little trouble, at the age of five or six, and they develop into perfectly adequate readers. But I believe these same children, if raised to read natively, might have learned to read even *more* easily, and they would have learned at the age of two or three years. They would have found the process of learning more fun and more intuitive, and I think most children would become even *better* lifelong readers if they learned natively. And don't forget that early readers have the gift of several additional years to *use* their ability to read; they get to enjoy reading, and to share reading with their parents, long before they ever enter school. Through their reading they can learn many things during their early years, while other children are still preliterate. Early readers end up getting an enormous head start in their intellectual development. So native reading can be beneficial even for children who do fine with current practices.

But there are also many children who currently struggle when they learn to read. I think that many, if not most, of these children could have read easily and well if only they had learned to read earlier, when they were more neurologically receptive to the low-level structure of language. For some children, five or six years old may already be too late to ever develop an intuitive grasp of the quirks of the written word. And even if they can eventually master reading, it comes at a great cost, in effort and frustration—a cost that could have been avoided if only they had learned earlier—just as many adults can eventually attain proficiency in a foreign language, but only after tremendous effort and years of practice; and, for many people, even after an enormous investment of effort and time, true native fluency remains unobtainable.

Misconception #7: Only stay-at-home parents have the time to teach native reading.

I don't believe a child needs a stay-at-home father or mother in order to learn to read natively, but I must admit that this misconception may hold a grain of truth. This is a tricky subject and deserves some discussion. The experience of my own family is in teaching native reading with parents as the nearly-exclusive caregivers for our children during their first years. Through the sometimes complicated juggling and coordination of work schedules, and also as a result of some serious professional sacrifices and outright career hiatuses by their parents, my children always had at least one parent at home with them until they were each three years old and started preschool. Some wonderful in-home babysitters for a few hours a week, and an occasional hour in drop-in YMCA childcare while either their mother or I got some much-needed exercise—these were the only exceptions to their parental care. So, despite their unique personalities and their individual courses of development, both of my children were very proficient native readers before they "left the nest" and entered an institutional childcare or preschool environment.

The decision to structure our family life this way was certainly partly selfish; their mother and I simply did not want to miss any of our children's first miraculous years, not the way many parents do these days. We wanted to be the ones who witnessed their first smiles, their first steps, and their first words; not someone paid by the hour—someone who, however wonderful, would probably disappear from our child's life soon after witnessing these milestones. The decision to parent our children this way was also driven by our belief that we would be more responsive to our children's needs than hired care would be. We felt that we could give our children a better start, both emotionally and intellectually, during their important first years of life.

Having taken time off from my own career in order to care for my young children, I am definitely not one to minimize the difficulty of this choice. There are serious consequences, financial and psychological, that follow from making the quality of your child's early years a priority. But, for me, the decision to bring a child into the world makes that child's welfare the primary responsibility of the parents—far more important than their devotion to their careers, and *vastly* more important than the type of vacations they take, or the luxury of the cars they drive. While it may be frustrating and humbling perhaps, a career certainly can be resumed after a hiatus, or an entirely new career can be started. In contrast, the first years of your child's life are uniquely important and completely unrecoverable, both for your child and for you.

That said, I do believe native reading *can* be successfully taught to children whose parents are both frequently away working. However, I think that at the present time, both because of common practical limitations of childcare-for-hire and also because of more fundamental difficulties, paid childcare will generally be a disadvantage in teaching native reading to your child.

To start with, any honest assessment of a sampling of childcare centers makes perfectly plain that while many people who work in childcare are wonderful caregivers, there are also some who are not. Caring for children is all too often a poorly-paid job, and often one where little education and experience are required. While many people work in childcare *despite* this, choosing to do so out of a genuine love of caring for children, there are others who do the work simply because there is a great demand for inexpensive childcare. It may well be one of the few jobs for which they can actually get hired. In some child-care settings there are a shocking number of "teachers" with *very* sparse education and limited literacy. (In fact, an unsettling consequence of successfully raising a native reader is that you will not infrequently meet adults, including adults whose job is ostensibly to teach children, who are considerably less literate than your three-year-old.) It's perfectly true that some of these same childcare workers may be wonderful at supporting your child's emotional development, *but they cannot do much for your child's intellectual development, and why would you settle for less than both?*

It is also undeniable that, although for the child it amounts mostly to fun and games, creating a richly-correlated native-reading environment requires considerable work by the parent, and this is similarly true for any caregiver who is substituted for a parent. Much of this work is best done on a one-on-one basis. There is no way around the fact that caregivers who cannot give a great deal of one-on-one attention to your child are simply not in a position to adapt their methods to your child's unique personality, and to your child's specific abilities and strengths. Because of the typical ratio of teachers to children in most institutional childcare settings, few of the teachers can possibly know, for example, your child's favorite books, or your child's favorite games. They are unlikely to know at what level your child's understanding is *today*, after the breakthroughs of just yesterday. It is very hard for a teacher with a whole classroom of kids to pick up a favorite activity right where it left off yesterday, the way a parent easily can. For example, even well-meaning teachers who attempt to follow native-reading techniques could risk being counterproductive if they *bore* your child because they mistakenly focus on single-letter play when, in fact, your child has advanced into whole words and is, therefore, currently much more engaged by play of greater complexity—games involving advanced words, rhyming play, and stories. It can be easy for such a teacher to mistake indifference and boredom for inability, to mistakenly conclude that your child cannot even grasp single letters, when they are actually woefully underestimating your child's level of understanding.

Someday, I believe it should be possible, with considerable care and thought, to structure an institutional childcare setting in such a way that it very successfully promotes native reading. Whether such a setting can approach the outcome of the best parent-led teaching is something I am less sure of. But for now there remains the simple disadvantage that, until native reading becomes quite common, few childcare centers will have any knowledge of the theory or of the method. And I suspect it may well take some time, even after two and three-year-old readers become fairly commonplace, before most childcare professionals embrace native reading. You certainly could loan this book to your child's teachers, and express your interest that they give the methods a try. But because native reading will seem like more work for them—and teaching native reading *does* involve more work, particularly more one-on-one attention, than most childcare centers are prepared to give—I unfortunately expect that most of your child's teachers will have the tendency to be hostile to the idea, given their conflicts of interest. Parents who can afford an intelligent, caring, and reliable in-home babysitter or nanny are probably in the best position—after parents who are home with their children—to successfully help their children become native readers. By the way, by a "reliable" babysitter, I don't simply mean someone who shows up on time. I mean a babysitter who is a reliable, trusted, and loved part of your child's life. Even if each is intelligent and well-meaning, a series of different babysitters cobbled together for different days of the week, or a succession of wonderful but short-term nannies, will not replace a steadier presence. If children are constantly rebuilding their trust and their emotional relationship with a caregiver, they cannot be expected to have the same level of attention for other tasks.

I am not saying, of course, that there won't be rare exceptions to this—the phenomenal babysitter your child takes to immediately, who finds the concept of native reading interesting and exciting, and who might even be better than you at incorporating the specific techniques into wonderfully creative and intellectually-stimulating play—I'm just saying such exceptions are likely to be just that: exceptions, and probably rare ones at that. (And if you *are* lucky enough to find such a babysitter-from-heaven, you had better keep it quiet. In my experience, they're in such a limited supply that there are many parents out there who would love to steal him or her away!)

So, again, I don't think you have to be a stay-at-home parent for your child to learn to read natively. However, because of all these factors, I do expect that the children who have the greatest success with the methods of this book—those who start reading natively at the earliest age and with the least effort—will usually be children whose parents have made spending time with their family an unequivocal priority.

Can Native Reading
Prevent Dyslexia?

Dyslexia is often given as the reason for why some children are late readers. I believe that, for many cases of dyslexia, this belief may be precisely backwards. To put this idea as clearly as possible:

I believe that many children are dyslexic *because they are late readers.*

That is, I believe dyslexia is often an *effect* of late reading, rather than the cause of it.

I suspect that this will be a controversial idea for some people. As someone trained as a scientist, I also readily admit that this idea is only a hypothesis, and a speculative one at that. But remember that every good idea starts out as speculation (as do bad ideas, to be sure). Because I find the logic supporting the idea that late reading may lead to dyslexia so compelling, I felt I had to devote a separate chapter to it in this book. Many common features of dyslexia are explained by this idea: including the particular language difficulties many dyslexics have and which children are most likely to suffer from it. And if the hypothesis is true, even if for just some fraction of cases of dyslexia, it further implies that:

> Learning to read natively, at an earlier age than is considered normal today, may *prevent* many cases of dyslexia.

Obviously, the possibility that a simple change in the way we teach children to read may prevent a frustrating and, in some cases, debilitating learning disability is potentially very important. Especially when that same change—teaching children to read natively—is also beneficial for children who are not likely to suffer from dyslexia even with current practices. There is no downside at all.

I also believe this developmental explanation of the origin of dyslexia helps explain the way that dyslexia is, in many ways, a *smart* disease, in a very deep sense of the word. And this helps account for the fact that, frequently, people who are dyslexic are also extremely intelligent.

I have a personal interest in this aspect of dyslexia because, though I am not myself dyslexic, I had a roommate in college who was. In fact, it was this friendship that first got me to think about reading in a fundamental way. In general, reading for me was something that came fairly easily, but, for my roommate, writing and reading were a frustrating agony. Yet, he was so eloquent in conversation, even on the sort of abstract and difficult topics that would challenge many perfectly-fluent readers. It was also fascinating because, while writing a paper for an English class was a slow and agonizing task for him, in the more stylized and simplified language of computer programming my roommate was a virtual genius. It was because of the contrast to my roommate's experience that I first appreciated—or even noticed, really—my own relative ease and facility with reading. I first began to think critically about cognitive aspects of reading.

At this same time, I was also studying topics like logic, computer science, evolutionary biology, and neuroscience; so I had some interesting and important tools with which to think about reading. But even more illuminating was the fact that I also began taking French in college. French was a language I had never studied before. My lack of concentration and my halting comprehension in this new language struck me as very similar to my roommate's struggles in written English. I had a running joke that, in French, *I* was dyslexic. It wasn't much more than an observation and a joke at the time, but I now feel, in light of the theory of native reading, that the joke might have contained a very important truth.

To see this, it is important to remember that the spoken and written forms of a language are deeply related; they are just two different forms of the same language, after all, and they have almost entirely analogous regularities and analogous quirks. But the analogy is *not* exact. There are some features of the written language that have no analogue in the spoken language at all. Even where the correspondence is fairly close, there still remain particular aspects that are only found in the written form of a language. *And it is precisely these novel features of written language—rather than the arguably hardest parts of language—which are some of the most common stumbling blocks for dyslexics.*

Many dyslexics, in fact, are perfectly adept at the harder aspects of language. They can do as well as anybody at such complex tasks as properly conjugating irregular verbs and correctly using complex syntactical forms. In contrast, distinguishing a "d" from a "b", a fundamentally simple task, can be bafflingly difficult. There is real irony, even tragedy, in the struggle that dyslexics have in distinguishing a "d" from a "b": while this is a struggle that often makes them feel dumb, I believe that the core of the problem is that they are, developmentally speaking, *already too smart* when they learn these quirks of reading and writing. The problem is not the complexity of the task, the problem is that they are already *masters* of spoken language by the time they encounter writing. Their brains do not expect to have low-level novelties of language introduced at this point in their development. At this point they are already concerned with meaning and nuance in language, with telling stories and conversing with their friends, with furthering their already well-developed social interests by *using* language; these are all very smart and complex tasks.

In contrast, the simple difference between a "d" and a "b" is a new quirk of the written form of language. You see, these two letters are *mirror images* of each other, something with no real analogy in spoken language. And, moreover, mirror symmetry is something that a five-year-old has already learned to regard, at an almost instinctive level, as *usually meaningless*. Your best friend facing to the right and your best friend facing to the left is still your best friend, a door that opens to the right and a door that opens to the left is still just a door; we generally don't even notice such mirror-symmetric differences. In fact, it is useful and smart to learn to ignore them, *to learn to not even see them*, which is what our brains generally do. But, then, long after this useful cognitive strategy has been acquired, a child is confronted by written language where, suddenly, "d" and "b" have entirely different meanings, and "dog" and "bog" are two entirely different words.

Many other aspects of written English which are particular difficulties for many dyslexics are, similarly, other symmetries or near-symmetries of letters: for example, "p" and "q", another mirror symmetry; "u" and "n", a case of rotational symmetry; and "n" and "m" or "v" and "w", which display a variant of another type of symmetry usually called translational or iterative symmetry. Dyslexics also often have problems with the proper usage of capital and lowercase letters, and with silent letters and other idiosyncrasies of spelling (like the way "c" and "s" can make the same sound, but so can "c" and "k").

What unites all these problems is not that they are particularly hard problems, what unites them is that they are problems that have no analogy in the spoken language. They are problems at a basic, building-block level of language—a level that, in the *spoken* language, five-year-olds have already mastered. They have been masters of this fundamental level of speech for many years, in fact. But, with the typical late introduction of reading, most children find themselves, at the age of five or six, suddenly and unexpectedly confronting these low-level complexities of *written* language. Often, children at this age are also, developmentally speaking, *appropriately* uninterested: as they are already masters of low-level spoken language and of low-level visual interpretation, a continued interest in these subjects would be superfluous. Therefore, when the artificial technology of writing is introduced at this late stage of cognitive development, it's perfectly natural that children are often easily frustrated by it. It is deeply unnatural to be forced to concentrate on such low-level tasks of perception at this point in childhood. At five years old, children are long past the age of babbling, they already have large vocabularies, and some of their delight in the rhyming absurdities of Dr. Seuss may already be fading. Rather, they want stories with meaning and social nuance; they are busy forging relationships with peers. At this age they are also usually in the challenging and interesting new environment of school. Children in school are, therefore, understandably frustrated to find themselves being grilled on the quirky mechanics of the lowest level of written English— they are, after all, already fully fluent in spoken English.

But why do some children become dyslexic and others not? Under current educational practices, most children eventually adequately get the hang of the new quirks of written language.

Children often do go through a stage where they occasionally reverse letters, struggle with capitalization, and make other "dyslexic-like" mistakes. It can be quite a struggle indeed to learn to read—and comprehension especially can remain marginal for many children—but, still, it is only a minority of children that end up categorized as dyslexic. This is actually exactly what you would expect, given the natural genetic and environmental variation among individuals. Children certainly vary, both in the timing of their optimal window for language acquisition, and in the length and shape of this developmental window of best opportunity. Children's environments also differ in subtle ways. For example, children who have merely *heard* a foreign language consistently during infancy, even though they didn't actually learn to speak it at the time, can often learn it more easily when they study it later in life. In particular, they are often better able to speak this language without any discernable accent, compared to people who were never exposed to the language as infants. Similarly, I believe that part of the reason parental literacy is important, and much of why it accurately predicts a child's success reading in school, is because children with literate parents generally have had at least some exposure to letters and words from an early age (although their environment is only rarely correlated enough to allow them to read natively and spontaneously before school).

At the time they start school, children certainly vary in their neural flexibility for tasks such as learning low-level aspects of language processing, and of visual processing, too. With non-native-reading practices, what children actually need to do is particularly difficult: they need to *un*learn much of what they already know about language and cognitively retrain themselves at a low neurological level in order to acquire the fundamentals of the written word. Currently, many children are first consistently introduced to written language as late as five years of age, or even later. Those children who retain sufficient cognitive flexibility at this age—even though it's far less flexibility than they had a few years earlier—these children end up reading "normally". (Although reading "normally" entails much more struggle, and deficits in comprehension, when compared to children who learned to read more natively when they were younger.) But children who, unfortunately, do not retain sufficient neural flexibility at five years of age are labeled "dyslexic". At best these children often remain baffled and frustrated by the written word for many years. At worst, they continue to have considerable difficulty reading and writing for the rest of their lives.

This is the native-reading theory of dyslexia. If many cases of dyslexia are indeed caused by introducing reading too late, an obvious possibility presents itself: many cases of dyslexia might be easily and automatically prevented if only children were taught to read natively. Nearly all children naturally master the essentials of *spoken* language before they are three years old. Native reading says this is also the time when children are best able to master the fundamentals of *written* language. They just need to be given the proper correlative environment that the native-reading techniques provide. They need an environment where the relationship of spoken and written language is clear and intuitive for a child, as it is in a native-reading home. In this way, rather than struggling with the quirks of reading and writing throughout their life, native readers instead have a deep, low-level *feel* for language, both spoken *and* written. Long before school, native readers gain an almost visceral fluency for language in all of its forms, and they will enjoy this advantage for the rest of their lives.

EIGHT

What Native Reading
Will Give to Your Child

Having a child who reads fluently at the age of two or three is certainly a wonderful thing in itself, but simply reading earlier is not what native reading is all about. Native reading is about the ease with which children learn to read when they learn before they are three. It's about their joy in the process. And it's about the benefits their deep literacy will bring them later in life.

Native reading is about making sure that the written word—one of the most ubiquitous and necessary technologies of modern life—is effortlessly intuitive for your child. When you teach your children to read natively, you are making sure that written language is *not* a technology that your children will trip over and struggle with for years, even through their entire lives. By learning to read early, and more naturally, children do not get stuck in the mechanics of reading. Instead, the correlation between written language and spoken language becomes so deeply known to them that, in a real sense, they see right through the symbols of writing. They see directly into the *meaning* of words. Native readers' deep fluency makes reading comprehension essentially automatic, rather than a secondary cognitive step that often remains sketchy at best, even into adulthood (as I know well, having taught many college undergraduates). For native readers, the mechanics of reading are as natural and effortless as the mechanics of speech. Their minds are free to concentrate on the *meaning* of the words, free to truly comprehend language and better able to use it effectively.

Learning to read is not an end in itself. The written word is one of the essential channels through which vast expanses of knowledge are accessed. By reading earlier, your child will certainly get a great head start on this process. That, in itself, is an important advantage. But much more important is the fact that when children read with ease and with good comprehension, all their subsequent learning comes more easily, too. Good readers learn with less cost—in time, effort, and frustration—and with more comprehension and intellectual benefit. The whole process of learning becomes more rewarding this way. Children who enter school already able to read fluently will generally find their lessons more fun, more interesting, and less frustrating. They'll get more out of their education, and they will gain an important sense of intellectual self-confidence that will stay with them throughout life. *This* is what native reading is all about.

In contrast, many children today are introduced to reading too late. They are left to struggle with a non-native, laborious grasp of the low-level mechanics of reading. Late readers often have to expend great effort to master silent "e"s and hard "c"s, basic punctuation, capitalization, and other quirks of written language, despite the relative simplicity of these things. These children may stumble for years over words, often to their great embarrassment. They frequently find themselves being frustrated by all the red ink on their spelling work. Children who read non-natively can easily begin to hate school. They may even start to think of themselves as stupid. It is common for late-reading children to slowly and arduously sound out a long word when they read, mispronouncing the word very badly, *despite the fact that they are completely familiar with the same word when it's spoken.* When this happens, many times these children obviously never realize that it is the same word, so familiar to them in speech. No wonder many children have such poor reading comprehension. These children are working hard, and they are often very intelligent; the problem is that their intelligence is largely focused on the *mechanics* of the written word.

If only they had learned to read earlier, not only would they have mastered these mechanics long before school, but the quirky mechanics of writing would generally be something that they *would not even notice*. It would be effortless for them, if only they had learned to read when they were behaviorally and neurobiologically most receptive to the fundamentals of language—if only they had learned to read in the way they learned to speak. It is such a wasted opportunity. Avoiding this waste and needless struggle is what native reading is all about.

On the subject of wasted opportunities, I have hopes that native reading will eventually provide another benefit, not just to the individual child, but to the wider society. Native reading, when it becomes sufficiently widespread, may help to narrow some of the troubling and persistent educational gaps among children in our society. Specifically, I hope the introduction of native reading will eventually narrow the gap between those children who were lucky enough to be born into families with advantages of wealth and education and those children who were not so fortunate. I believe the existence of such educational achievement gaps, and their stubborn persistence, may be partly explained by the fact that poor children are frequently raised in homes where there is very little reading at all. A few of these children certainly manage to catch up, despite their disadvantages. With the help of devoted parents and teachers, a few disadvantaged children even manage to outshine their more fortunate peers. But many more poor children are left to struggle with a very non-native facility with the written word, sometimes for their entire lives. They therefore suffer more frequently and more severely from dyslexia and from other language-based learning disabilities. Even much later in their schooling, these children tend to find reading and learning much more work, and much less rewarding, in comparison to children who were early readers. I hope that native reading will provide a simple method—a method that's not expensive and is open to any literate parent—that will unlock more of the intellectual potential all children have.

I am aware that, in the short term, the introduction of native reading is unlikely to noticeably decrease educational inequity. To start with, the early adopters of native reading will be those parents who have the time and the inclination to read a book like this. Such parents are likely to be more literate, more educated, and, if not necessarily wealthy, still probably less likely to be extremely poor. But native reading is fundamentally different from many of the advantages wealthy parents can provide for their children; it's not like private school, or private tutoring, or SAT-prep coaching. Helping your child to be a native reader is not a question of money. None of the techniques of native reading require an advanced degree or any sort of expensive equipment. To teach native reading what you need is energy, patience, and a willingness to play thoughtfully with your child. You have to value your child's early development. The only materials required are things which are already found in most loving homes. You need books, paper, crayons, and a few toys. Most importantly, you need parents who love their children and who make their children's learning and happiness a priority.

In fact, because it is very difficult to replace a parent's role in a child's early development, the people who might have the most difficult time raising native readers may actually be some of the wealthiest. Those parents whose days are dominated by the priorities of their careers, while leaving their children's early development to professional childcare, will have more difficulty providing the consistently supportive environment that best fosters native reading. And just as these high-income, but harried, parents may miss their child's first words, or first steps, they are also likely to miss the sometimes subtle signs of progress towards native reading—progress which can be reinforced best if the signs are immediately recognized. Even with the best professional childcare, caregivers are often constantly turning over, or are undereducated, or, in many cases, both. While I don't think it is impossible to create a professional childcare environment that effectively supports native reading—and creating such an environment is, indeed, a priority in order to help children whose parents are unable to perform the teaching role themselves—I do not think it will be an easy task, either. The empathy, trust, and long-term involvement of a loving parent are fundamentally impossible to replace. To make up for this disadvantage, a successful institutional setting would have to be very well designed, and very well implemented. For this reason, native reading will come most naturally for children whose mothers and fathers have made difficult sacrifices in their careers in order to best care for their children during the crucial first years of life.

These native-reading families may not drive luxury automobiles, and they will probably spend less money at the dry cleaners, but their children will be deeply and fluently literate—one of the essential foundations of intelligence—not only when they are very young, but throughout their schooling, into college, and for the rest of their lives.

NOTES

This book is not, by any means, intended to be a review of the literature on reading acquisition in children; rather, it is primarily and directly based on my firsthand experience helping my own children learn to read natively. My main goal was to describe the methods I developed to successfully encourage their early native reading. But there are many sources, both general and specific, which have inspired me, informed me, and helped me to articulate my methods. Therefore, I have included these notes after the main text. In part, they are here to reference particular sources of interest while, at the same time, avoiding needless encumbrance of the main text. These notes are also a place to mention ideas, implications, and tangents which—while not essential to the book or necessary to successfully use its methods to teach native reading—I believe have relevance and might be of interest to those curious about where the theory of native reading came from. As you'll see, the main intellectual threads which form the basis of the theory of native reading spring not from traditional work in child development, but rather from neuroscience, evolutionary biology, and computer science. The relevance of computer science in understanding child development may surprise some people, but I believe one of the most important results of artificial intelligence research is that because of work in this field we've begun to gain a deeper understanding and appreciation of *natural* intelligence.

These notes are organized by the chapter where the topics appear in the text, and are referenced by the quoted passage from the main text to which each note refers. There are no references to the notes in the main text, therefore there are three strategies for using these notes: (1) ignore them completely, and stick to the main text; (2) keep a finger or bookmark in the notes and check back now and again to read the notes more or less as each quoted passage is encountered; or (3) read the main text without troubling with the notes, and then go on to read the notes in a single session, either after completing each chapter of the main text, or even after reading the entire main text. With the last strategy, the notes will serve as a kind of review of the topics, as well as a more advanced and wide-ranging "Volume 2" of sorts. I believe that each of these strategies represents a perfectly reasonable choice.

Notes to Chapter 2. The Correlation Method of Native Reading

page 15 *All those tiny little children <u>speaking perfect French</u>!* Even more funny is the feeling a traveler can have at the apparent absurdity of speaking to, say, a dog in French—even the dogs are smarter than you!

page 17 *The way to create the proper environment for native reading is to make a child's world rich in <u>correlations</u> between spoken language and written language.*" I want to acknowledge here an intellectual debt to the work of Gerald Edelman and his coworkers at The Neurosciences Institute for impressing on me the fundamental importance of correlation in learning. When I was a graduate student at Princeton University, I was invited to give a talk at The Neurosciences Institute. My visit there was very wide-ranging and intellectually stimulating and it had a great influence on my later thinking. The theoretical and experimental neuroscientific results I encountered at the Institute were often on my mind when, only about a year later, my son was born and I began watching him learn about his world.

The work of Edelman is most relevant, too, in gaining an understanding into the effortless way reading develops when taught natively. His view of the brain is one where connections between neurons are strengthened when their responses are correlated. Roughly put, by doing this the brain is organizing itself, developing a minimally-complex model of the world, learning about relationships in the environment, and reducing the redundancy of its representation of the world. (Overall, it is a very "bottom up" approach: where simple low-level rules organize neural resources into higher-level understanding. I believe that, in contrast, much of traditional developmental psychology takes far too much of a "top down" approach; this is, to some extent, a vestige of its historical roots in metaphysical philosophy.)

For those phenomena which are closely related and naturally correlated in their structure—as spoken language and written language are—the brain creates correlated neural structures that are a kind of internal representation, or map, of the learned related tasks. Again, this comes from the bottom up: it's not that a child concludes, in a deductive way, that the two forms of language are related; rather, the low-level structure of the brain automatically encodes the correlation, and the knowledge thus comes about inductively (later, an explicit, more "deductive", understanding of the correlative relationship may certainly develop, but this is really a relatively minor intellectual elaboration, rather than the core of intelligence; this is the issue that many developmental psychologists continue to confuse, often actually getting the relative importance of implicit and explicit understanding precisely backwards, in my opinion).

There is an important incentive to begin to stabilize, to nail down, these internal neural maps of the world when they have reached a high degree of accuracy. This is what leads to the windows of opportunity in childhood neurodevelopment (or, in the more worry-provoking, traditional terminology, "critical periods" in development). For example, once you've learned and essentially mastered understanding speech and speaking yourself, your brain has every incentive to consolidate and "harden" that knowledge, working to reduce the redundancy of its neural representation of this knowledge, and fixing it, so you can get on to learning other tasks. By hardening and even fixing the lower level of language (the phonemes and basic syntactical rules, for example) the brain can then turn its attention to the metalevel of *using* language: telling stories, perceiving nuances of meaning, gossiping with peers. The problem with current educational practice is that it's at this late point in a child's development when reading is typically first introduced in a consistent way.

Reading this late, at around five years old, may also throw a child's brain for a particular loop because the relevant information comes in by *a totally different perceptual channel*: reading is entirely visual, while speech is almost entirely auditory. Suddenly the brain has to forge new low-level connections: relating the *sounds* of the already unconsciously-perceived phonemes with the letters of written language that it takes in *visually*. It is a testament to the flexibility and sheer power of the human brain that children usually manage to achieve these connections, albeit after considerable frustration, when learning to read so late. (As I detail in Chapter 7, however, I think that some children *cannot* easily manage the difficult task of learning to read separately and later—so long after they learned to speak—and that this cognitive impasse is expressed in their dyslexia.)

However, even when reading *is* successfully acquired in kindergarten and later, I think the neural representations of language that result are likely to be less efficient—fundamentally more redundant—than when a child learns to read natively. A five-year-old learning to read is cognitively forced to cobble together an ad-hoc representation of the written language and attempt to make efficient connections with an already advanced and consolidated representation of oral language. And this child has the additional complication that the two forms of language arrive through distinct channels of perception. It will be interesting, when native reading becomes more common, to see whether functional brain imaging studies demonstrate that native readers possess a deeper connection between the written and spoken language centers of the brain—inasmuch as they may be separable at all—and also whether native readers generally have richer and more efficient connections between their auditory and visual perceptual processing regions.

In addition to Edelman and his coworkers, there are many other scientists whose work has had an important influence on my conception of learning, and this is a good place to mention a few more: Teuvo Kohonen and his work on topological feature maps, a most elegant and simple way of modeling heuristic mapping; David Hubel and Torstin Wiesel and their classic work on the developmental neurophysiology of vision (for which they won a well-deserved Nobel prize); also, Douglas Hofstadter's book *Godel, Escher, Bach: An Eternal Golden Braid* (Basic Books) had a great influence on my thinking about mechanisms of learning, and about the related concepts of mappings, isomorphisms, and analogies, ever since I first read it when I was about twenty years old. None of these workers had much, if anything, to say on reading acquisition specifically, but I thought often of their more general theories of learning and neurodevelopment as I developed my own particular methods of teaching reading—as I worked to develop techniques that made the best use of the brain's natural abilities.

Finally, in my thinking about child development there is a somewhat oblique, but I think still important, influence from the work of the writer Bruce Chatwin, especially his book *The Songlines.* This book, in its pointillist manner, manages to sketch out a poetic theory on the origins of human language—both on the origin of language in every individual's early development, and on the advent of language in the prehistory of our species.

page 23 *Even two-year-olds generally have the fully-developed visual system and more than enough cognitive capacity to allow them to read easily, so long as their environment properly fosters native reading.* Here is a good place to mention the fact that there are some pretty weird, and largely unsupported, "folk theories" about child development in circulation out there. One I have come across is the notion that the eye muscles of young children are not sufficiently developed to allow reading before the age of five, or thereabouts. Clearly my children provide two "existence proofs" that this notion is false, at least for some children. (And the existence of many other early readers, while still statistically rare, adds much more empirical weight to the argument against the "eye-muscle theory".)

This "eye-muscle theory" seems to crop up in the educational community in particular. While there probably are some people who honestly believe this theory is true, to put it somewhat undiplomatically, I think its popularity is also due to the fact that it provides a scientific-sounding excuse for poor early academic performance in schools.

The "eye-muscle theory", of course, shows profound evolutionary and developmental ignorance. While it is true that much of neurodevelopment is still characterized by continuing refinement as late as five years old (although much of the refinement is actually pretty minor by this late point), the development of the visual system is very largely complete much earlier in development. In fact, the classic and insightful work of David Hubel and Torstin Wiesel firmly established the basics of this developmental fact over fifty years ago. Yet pseudoscientific folk notions live on.

The evolutionary ignorance of the "eye-muscle theory" is particularly astonishing. As soon as a child is independently mobile—that is, by the age of about twelve months—to expect anything less than highly-developed eye-muscle coordination, quite good binocular convergence and tracking, and excellent visual acuity is evolutionarily absurd. Even without knowing the details of neurodevelopment, upon a little reflection it should be obvious that any such visual deficiency at the age of independent mobility would be *very* strongly selected against in the human population. A child who was toddling about with such visual deficiencies would have been very "easy pickings" for the various predators in our species' history, as well as being vulnerable to all sorts of accidental injuries.

Of course, just common-sense observation of a few 18-month-old children makes their visual abilities perfectly clear. Such toddlers walk around quite successfully, navigating about their complex environment. They visually track moving objects. They can make eye contact with you from across the room, and hold it easily as they cruise along towards you. They also often do things like getting fascinated by a tiny ant crawling along the pavement, watching it and commenting on its every move, following the miniscule animal expertly with their gaze until it disappears into the grass. This sort of simple observation gives obvious evidence of the high degree of visual system development and eye-muscle coordination in even a very young child.

Any "insufficiency of gaze" or "coordination deficit" for reading that poorly-designed studies of children may show has, I believe, a simple explanation. If a child has no idea what text is for, doesn't even recognize it as important, and does not know simple facts like, for example, how it flows (in English) from left to right, then I am sure that, experimentally, that child will not track a line of text at all like a reader does. But when such a child does not track text smoothly it is generally simply because they lack the knowledge and the motivation to do so, not because they lack the low-level visual ability. (Even mountains of experimental data can leave you ignorant, by the way, if you have the wrong theory. Tycho Brahe demonstrated this nicely at the dawn of modern science nearly five hundred years ago: he collected vast amounts of data of unprecedented accuracy on planetary movements over his long astronomical career, refining the then-dominant Ptolmeic models of the heavens, but he apparently couldn't bear the thought of putting the sun at the center.)

Notes to Chapter 3. Learning to be a Native Reader is Fun!

page 27 *A child's ability to acquire language should be optimal before the age of three because this is the age when children naturally master spoken language—and remember, for countless human generations before just the last hundred years or so, spoken language was the only language a person typically learned. Remember, too, that just a few hundred years before that, nearly everywhere across the world, reading was something that only a tiny percentage of educated monks and scribes ever learned at all.* This novelty of the written word in human history necessarily implies that there is no reason at all, from an evolutionary perspective, to expect there to be a later optimal window for reading acquisition. And yet many educational professionals seem to irrationally expect exactly such a thing. In fact, there is no reason to expect any specifically-evolved aptitude for reading at *any* time in development. Our ability to read is an "accidental" result of our evolved aptitude for spoken language, along with our great cognitive flexibility—adaptations which together allow us to extend our language ability to the evolutionarily-recent technology of the written word.

Because our aptitude for language acquisition is greatest in our earliest years—as demonstrated by our effortless ability to acquire spoken language as very young children—and, further, as our cognitive flexibility is generally also greatest when we are young (and then decreases as we age), there is every reason to expect that most children, given the appropriate environment, will learn written language most easily and deeply if they begin the process during their first three years of life.

This same evolutionary consideration of reading gives substantial insight into the variable aptitude for reading that is found in different children. Every trait exhibits variation, but traits that are not under strong selection are likely to be especially variable. Therefore, it is not surprising that children—in any learning environment, including a native-reading environment—will display considerable variation in the trajectory and timing of their ability to read. This diversity is a major reason why I emphasize that you should not push a child who seems to be making slow progress, and it's also why you should not worry if your child's path to reading shows individual quirks that you do not find in this book. Your child might start independent reading at three, or he or she may well be reading fluently before the age of two. I don't think you should be surprised either way. This expected variability is the reason I don't include any timetable for learning to read in this book. Children will "get it" when they are ready; but when they are raised in a native-reading home, they will generally get it much earlier and more easily than is typical of children who learn to read non-natively.

By the way, I don't believe that (so long as the home is a supportive, native-reading environment) the age at which your children first read is likely to say much about their overall intelligence. I do, however, think that a child's unique trajectory may well say something about that child's *particular* intellectual strengths. For example, I don't think my son is, in a general way, any smarter than my daughter because he first read at around 18 months, compared to her 30 months. I do, however, find that he does seem to have particular skills with abstract concepts, and I think that these particular strengths are part of why he "got" reading so early. It is an oversimplification, but I would say that my son, now nearly nine, does seem to have a rather "analytical" mind. With a minimum of information he tends to be able to gain significant insight. My daughter's style of understanding is more what people term "synthetic"; she tends to learn by first gathering a great deal of experience over a greater period of time. Sometimes she doesn't make obvious progress at first, but then, much more suddenly, she effortlessly puts it all together, often displaying an immediate sophistication that can absolutely floor me. In this manner, her reading acquisition showed less obvious and gradual progression, and it came at a later age than with my son, but when my daughter suddenly "got" it, reading came almost saltationally, in a fairly complete form. Both ways of learning are highly effective, although one style or the other may sometimes be better suited to particular subjects.

Notes to Chapter 4. Creating the Native-reading Environment: 12 Techniques to Promote Native Reading for Your Child

page 31 *Regimented methods like that [phonics flashcards and the like] are, frankly, the way you'd teach a robot to read; and your child is not a robot.* When I speak disparagingly of robots, I am mostly speaking of a naïve view of learning in artificial intelligence research, which until comparatively recently was not entirely inaccurate. There is a much more nuanced movement in intelligence research in recent years. This research has, among other things, begun to appreciate the importance of implicit learning, rather than focusing on explicit learning, as much early AI work did.

The best way to explain what is meant by "implicit learning" is through an example. You can probably catch a ball pretty well, but really think for a moment about how you do this. Do you know the equation of the parabolic path of an object falling in a gravitational field, as well as how to make a complicated velocity-dependent correction for the frictional force of the air? Unless you have been in a physics class recently, you probably hardly know what I'm talking about. But as it turns out, if you can catch a ball success-fully, you *do* know this. You're rocket-scientist brilliant, you just don't know how to *describe* what you know—but then, if you can make 5 million dollars a year as a center fielder, who *cares* if you can describe what you know? In fact, it is true that knowing these things at a lower level—at a more fundamental, and not conscious, neural level—is *better* in many ways. In the case of the center fielder about to catch a fly ball, for example, knowing *implicitly* how to snag that fly ball leaves your head clear to think about other things, like throwing out that runner who is tagging up at third base! Analogously, understanding how to read at a deep, native level similarly lets a child focus on what is really important—the *meaning* of words—rather than consciously thinking about "ie" vs. "ei", or tripping over silent "e"s, or worrying over other such low-level mechanics.

It is also important, to stay with the center fielder example, that base-ball players (or children learning to play catch) don't learn the equations first and then somehow push them down into the subconscious. They learn the information inductively, by observation of the patterns of velocity and trajectory (without even having names for, or even explicit concepts of, things like "velocity" and "trajectory") in the course of their practice—in the course of their *play*.

page 33 *The point of these examples is that this [how an unfamiliar alphabet looks to an adult] is essentially what English (or any other language) looks like to a preliterate child. Abstract, meaningless, and probably frustrating to look at for very long.* The example of how an unfamiliar alphabet strikes an adult gives a hint of the difficulty a child has when first confronting the written word, but it actually underestimates that difficulty considerably. A literate adult already has many skills that a preliterate child does not possess. For example, you know that the unfamiliar symbols probably stand for *something*, and you probably already guess that they are, as in most common scripts, phonetic in nature. You also know how symbols are typically syntactically combined into words, how they are read in sequence, and how they are organized into lines (even if you may guess wrongly as to whether you should read left-to-right or right-to-left). A preliterate child has none of these skills. For all a preliterate child knows, a page of text might simply be an abstract picture with no beginning, no end, no phonetic interpretation, no relationship to the spoken word—in fact, no meaning at all. That said, learning to read is not actually a terribly *difficult* problem—not for a child easily capable of the amazingly complex task of learning to speak—but it is an extremely *non-intuitive* problem. The native-reading techniques work primarily by making the written word more intuitive for a child; they do this both by making the units of writing neurologically intuitive through letter play, for example, and more generally, by correlating reading acquisition with the deeply-related and intuitive task of learning to speak.

page 34 *But if you engage in letter play just about every day, even for just a few minutes, you will make the fundamental units of written language a recognizable and fun part of your child's world; letters will be familiar at a deep neurological level. And remember, your children use your behavior to learn what is important in their world, so if you show them that letters are important, they will take an interest, and they'll soak it right up.* When I say that letters will be deeply familiar neurologically, I mean it quite literally. In fact, I believe a native-reading child will actually see letters better. This statement will surprise, even dumbfound, some people. Many people think of their eyes (when they do at all) as simple cameras, but human vision is actually a very complex and adaptive process, as some common optical illusions clearly demonstrate. An accessible introduction to the neuropsychology of the visual system can be found in Richard Gregory's *Eye and Brain: The Psychology of Seeing* (Princeton University Press). Especially interesting, despite its being rather out-of-date, is the chapter entitled, "Do we have to learn how to see?" The answer, by the way, is that in large part we certainly do. Gregory also wrote another, somewhat less accessible, book with the wonderful and accurate title *The Intelligent Eye* (Weidenfield and Nicolson).

page 36 *Rather than looking like Greek probably looks to you, the building blocks of written language will then be deeply familiar to your child, and through your play, these symbols will already begin to be correlated with the spoken language that your child is soaking up, even in early infancy.* Years ago I spent part of two summers in Greece and had the sort of low-level neurological "aha!" experience that the native-reading techniques encourage in the mind of a child. Before arriving in Greece I had no formal training in the Greek language and, at first, even simple road signs and restaurant menus seemed almost completely inscrutable. To make sense of even the few words I knew, I had to painstakingly translate letter for letter before the meaning would slowly dawn on me. However, after a week or so I quite suddenly "got it". My brain, at a fairly low level, had mastered the simple mapping from the English alphabet to the closely-related (although superficially quite different-looking) Greek alphabet. I still had only a rudimentary understanding of grammar, tenses, and Greek vocabulary, but suddenly the spoken words I did know became crystal clear in their written form, too, and I was suddenly and happily aware of the many English-Greek cognate words, and also of the many commonly-used words that were borrowed from English and simply transliterated into Greek. It was as though a haze had lifted from my mind. After I had passed this threshold I could, for example, smile with immediate and effortless recognition when I boarded a particularly large Mediterranean ferry and noticed it was named the "Συπερφερρη". This is the sort of experience that the native-reading techniques make possible for your child; reading becomes something your child doesn't have to work at, a written word's meaning is just there for your child, plain as day.

(And, by the way, the Greek to English mapping is:
Σ → S, υ → u, π → p, ε → e, ρ → r, φ → f, ε → e, ρ → r, ρ → r, η → y.)

page 37 *They will 'babble' with their toys, they will enjoy nonsense words, they will, to an adult eye, spend a lot of time goofing around. This is not only all right, this is actually essential. Therefore, when your child turns all the words upside down on the refrigerator, do not 'correct' this behavior.* In theory there is the possibility of taking a tolerance for haphazard play too far. If children *only* looked at words in random orientation it would make learning more complicated than necessary, as they would then be learning to read not only in the normal manner, but also upside down, sideways, and every which way. And learning to read right side up is by far the most useful skill. But, in practice, there is little chance that such overly-random presentation will happen: every time you read a book to your child, you will do so with the book right side up; nearly every sign in a store and on a street will be right side up; the text on a television screen and on a computer screen are also right side up, etc.

So, practically speaking, adults need to work primarily at *restraining* their urge to "correct" the exploratory and experimental play of native-reading children. This is especially true because, when we were in school, reading was all-too-often presented to us as a serious and grown-up sort of activity; play or silliness or anything not "proper" was often actively discouraged, with the use of a great deal of red ink, even in the earliest grades. Older children may manage to learn *despite* this, but such a serious and dogmatic approach is totally inappropriate for a child of 1-3 years. The work of writers like Dr. Seuss, for example—where goofiness, wordplay, and downright nonsense are an essential part of the fun—this approach is far more engaging for a young child and, for that reason, far more conducive to learning to read.

page 38 *To be sure, with all its silent letters, and with the multiple sounds the same letter can make, this can be a somewhat complicated mapping in the English language.* This fact, that the mapping of spoken to written English does have some complications, is the main reason why I expect that native readers will typically progress similarly to the way my daughter did: while being extremely early and proficient by usual standards, their reading ability will parallel, but somewhat lag, their proficiency in the spoken language. So, for example, most native-reading children will probably start reading single words sometime after they are already speaking in complete sentences. It will range from this to the cases, like my son, where the development of speaking and reading are almost entirely parallel, with hardly any discernable lag at all.

The complicated nature of the phonetic mapping of spoken English to written English is, technically speaking, a result of what is usually termed the "redundancy" and the "degeneracy" of the mapping (note that the term "degeneracy" here does not have the "moral" connotation it has in common usage). These terms mean two things:

(1) A single sound can map to more than one letter, for example, the hard K sound can map to the letter "K", the "C", or even the "Qu".

(2) More than one sound can map to one letter, for example, the hard K sound can map to the letter "C", but the S sound can also map to the letter "C".

So, the mapping between writing and speech is somewhat tangled in both directions. Fortunately, spoken language is full of similar complications, too, so children have an extraordinary ability to learn complicated mappings like this. For example, from a child's perspective the sound "Mama" usually maps to their own mother, but children soon learn (sometimes after a bit of confusion) that the same sound can map to other mothers, too, particularly when uttered by other children. Similarly, it seldom takes children very long to learn that the sound "for" not only maps to the usual preposition "for" (with all its various shades of meanings), but that it also maps to the number "four", which sounds precisely the same; and even more complexly, the sound "for" additionally maps to many *parts* of words, as in the words "*for*get", "*for*k", "*for*tunately", and "*for*m", among many, many others. It is this natural genius every child has for mastering complicated mappings, full of degeneracy and redundancy, that is the envy of computer scientists attempting to make computers more intelligent. (By the way, much of the nonverbal world is also full of similar complications; transferability of "mapping" skills could be why early and advanced reading often correlates with achievement on tests that attempt to measure strictly visual intelligence, for example.)

The term "mapping" throughout this discussion, and elsewhere in the book, is a slightly relaxed analogue to the classical mapping of mathematics. In most of mathematics the unmodified term is only applied to mappings completely without degeneracy or redundancy (in comparison to English, for example, the Spanish of southern Spain, with relatively few silent letters, fewer letters that make the same sound, etc., is closer to a mathematical mapping between its spoken and written forms, although it is still not nearly close enough to count as a true mapping for the mathematician). There is also a mathematical concept which is related to, but slightly more complex than, the concept of mapping: this concept is termed "isomorphism". The power of the idea of isomorphism is wonderfully developed and discussed, in a brilliant and accessible manner, in the classic Douglas Hofstadter book which I've already mentioned in a note above: *Gödel, Escher, Bach: An Eternal Golden Braid* (Basic Books).

Both "mapping" and "isomorphism" have meanings approximate to the usual sense of the word "analogy". But my use of the more technical terms here is driven by the fact that the term analogy, in common speech, usually indicates a quite primitive correspondence between two simple objects.

Mappings (especially when relaxed from the strictest mathematical versions, and extended to allow cases with some degeneracy and redundancy) can also refer to more complex analogies between two different *sets* of objects, and analogies between sets of sets, too. In the case of isomorphism, the term also indicates that there are not only analogous objects or sets of objects, but there are also associated and corresponding *operations* on those objects or sets as well.

For example, the students of a classroom (for some school environments at least) are in some ways analogous to the lower-level workers in an office. The teacher is somewhat analogous to the office supervisor: they are both the boss. To some extent, a worker and a student can both "get in trouble with the boss" in the same way: the operation of "getting in trouble with the boss" applies with very much the same sense in both settings. Children who know enough to understand this isomorphism can then quite successfully use their own experience in school to interpret an adult conversation about a parent's frustration with a new supervisor. The isomorphism is not exact, of course, so a child may indeed gain a great deal of insight, but then may go on to furtively ask her mother, "Is Daddy going to flunk out of work?" (Of course, this, too, may be a pretty accurate description; with just the addition of "get fired" to her vocabulary, she may well be on the mark.)

The discussion of mappings and isomorphism is important in thinking about why early reading should be associated with intelligence later in development. There are at least four distinct conceptual reasons why one would expect earlier and more native reading to lead to greater lifelong intelligence. These reasons, while generally distinct, are certainly not mutually exclusive:

(1) The first advantage is that early reading gives rise to a "virtuous circle" of intellectual development in a young child—an example of positive feedback—where success breeds success. For example, children who read early possess another tool to analyze and practice language which helps them to better understand their world. Additionally, their reading *reinforces* (because of the fundamental correlation between the two forms of language) their growing ability in the spoken language, too. A simple example of this is the way native-reading children will often understand an advanced word in speech the very first time they hear it, because they previously encountered and learned that word in a book. There is a social aspect to this positive feedback as well: children who are earlier readers—and whose reading ability helps them understand speech, develops their vocabulary, and introduces them early to abstract conceptual thinking—these children

are likely to enjoy school, find it easy and rewarding, and generally feel it is something they are good at. This attitude, born from their social success with intellectual tasks like reading itself, as well as with all the subjects that proficient reading makes easier, will generally motivate them to further success. Success thus builds on success. This sort of social feedback is part of the argument that underlies the current fashion which finds many parents starting their children in kindergarten at six rather than at four or five: because these children are developmentally advanced, their early school experiences tend to be easier, and a child who starts at six is likely to be one of the more mature children, as well as simply the physically biggest. (I personally believe that for children taught to read at home this strategy may sometimes work—so long as everyone doesn't do it—but I think it might backfire for those children who are not taught anything about reading at home, who therefore are not introduced to reading until they start school as late as six or seven years old, when their cognitive flexibility is significantly diminished.)

(2) The second advantage of native reading for intelligence is that because the brain is optimally ready to learn languages before the age of three, a child can therefore learn more rapidly, more effortlessly, and more deeply at this age. Fundamentally this is due to the fact that, in our species' evolutionary history, spoken language (until just the last few generations) was the *only* language learned, and for most of this history it was surely learned as it is now, starting from early infancy, and with essential mastery of the principle linguistic structure before the age of three. Given the advantages language gives in communication, social coordination, strategic maneuvering, and many other areas, it is not at all surprising that selection pressures were sufficiently high to favor the nearly universal and early mastery of language. While there is certainly natural variation in intellectual development between individuals, and significant variability in when children master spoken language (see, for example, Thomas Sowell's interesting book *Late-Talking Children*, Basic Books), even accounting for this variation, nearly every child masters the essentials of speech *well before* they are typically taught to read today. There is, evolutionarily speaking, absolutely no reason to expect the ability to learn new fundamentals of language to persist later in life. While expansion of vocabulary, and other refinement, might continue throughout later development and into adulthood, before the advent of modern transportation very few individuals would typically even encounter foreign languages, much less have reason to gain fluency in them. So it is entirely expected that learning a foreign language should be easier for a child than for an adult. It is also not at all

surprising that if you do not learn a second language early in life, attaining "native" pronunciation and fluency is extremely hard. The linguistic task of learning to read (which is very isomorphic to the task of learning the spoken form of the same language), while novel in our evolutionary history, makes similar use of the brain's general ability to learn languages. Therefore, the optimal time to learn reading should be at about the same age as the optimal time to learn speech. There is absolutely no reason to expect some evolved second "reading window" at the age of five or six; reading is far too recent an innovation for such a coevolved second window to have been adaptively significant. We can read not because of a specifically evolved ability to do so, but because our evolved general abilities in language are sufficiently broad to allow the technological extension of reading. And these general abilities—particularly for picking up low-level, basic features of a language—are greatest early in childhood. Another reason that learning to read early is likely to be particularly beneficial is because the linguistic information of reading comes through an entirely different sensory channel—through sight—while spoken language is perceived through sound. While flexibility certainly remains, it is nonetheless true that basic sensory paths tend to be laid down very early in development; for some children, if they are not sufficiently introduced to a visual, written form of language early in their childhood, their linguistic abilities may develop quite neurally-isolated from their visual system. This is part of why I believe native reading may *prevent* many cases of dyslexia; and why I believe that, for many dyslexics, it is not that they read later because they are dyslexic, but that they are dyslexic because they read later. Most of the symptoms and paradoxes of dyslexia are exactly what would be expected from a brain without enough flexibility to make sufficient connections between its well-developed auditory linguistic representations and its new low-level visual representations for the written language. The non-intuitive abstract characters with which we write make this all the more difficult; the brain must *learn* to see, and it has already learned to generally ignore many of the niggling visual features (like mirror-symmetry) that become critically important in order to be fluently proficient at reading and writing.

(3) Another advantage of native reading is also due to the fact that oral and written language are highly-correlated systems (that is, very isomorphic). Because of their similar structures, learning oral and written language simultaneously should lead to a more compact, and therefore more efficient, representation of language in the brain. The way most children learn language now is by developing the fundamentals of spoken language skills separately and first, typically mastering the low-level aspects of language—

basic sentence structure, conjugation, vocabulary and syntax—well before the age of three. After children have learned the fundamentals of speech, there follows a period of several years where they concentrate on generally higher-level concepts of oral language: increasing vocabulary; learning about irony, humor, and other "storytelling" concepts; using language extensively for social interaction of increasing sophistication. Then, after *years* developing these higher-level language concepts, children suddenly, at the age of five or six, are brought back to square one and are belatedly given concentrated instruction on the low-level mechanics of *written* language: learning such things as the non-intuitive alphabetical symbols of writing, the plethora of nonstandard orthographical anomalies like silent letters, struggling to develop good instincts for the maze of redundancy and degeneracy in sound-to-letter mappings (and vice versa), and learning issues of capitalization, spacing, punctuation, and other foundational conventions of writing. To master the task of reading with comprehension, it is necessary for their brains to efficiently and fluidly link up these new low-level representations of written language with the low-level representations of oral language that were developed *years earlier* (and whose data were via an entirely different, auditory, sensory channel) and whose low-level neural representation has certainly become to some extent fixed, or "frozen in", since all that time passed. I think this (currently typical) non-native path by which children learn language probably results in much more separation of language function in the brain than is ideal, with relatively distinct centers of oral and written language (although there is probably great variation in this). So, not only do non-native readers have to go through the unnecessary struggle of learning many basic language skills twice, but the overall neural representation of language for non-native readers is then less efficient and more redundant because their course of development makes it difficult for late-reading children's brains to take full advantage of the simplifying isomorphism of oral and written language. Because of this inefficient redundancy, the neural representation of language will be less compact. Put simply, I think that non-native readers are likely to use *more* of their brain for language, and actually get *less* understanding for this extra effort and allocation. For example, my son could outspell me starting at about the age of three. He has only gotten better with time—though I am a decent speller—and he is able to spell correctly with such *ease*. I believe his instinctive feel for the quirks of English spelling is due to the fact that he has never really *not* known them. In contrast, though I learned to read quite easily around the age of five, I still have to *think more* about how to spell, and I still get caught up on some of the more bizarre orthographical irregularities (those "ie"s and "ei"s, for instance). My son often finds my difficulties quite hilarious, although he is old enough now (at eight) to be diplomatic about it. Still, it is hard for him to empathize with my struggle at a task that requires no effort at all for him. And his ability with spelling was developed without *any* explicit effort: it just came from his reading, not from any sort of regimented "spelling practice" at all. He is like the three-year-old girl who can't see why a foreign visitor trips over the irregular verbs that the *she doesn't even notice*, because she has never really *not* known them. A compact, efficient, near-optimal representation of language, with low-level and fluid connectivity between written and spoken words, doesn't just improve language skills: because of the substantial flexibility of allocation in the brain, an optimally compact "language center" also should leave more neural resources available for *every other kind of intellectual task*. Native reading is especially powerful because it does two things simultaneously: its compact neural representation of language frees up more of the brain for intellectual development *and* this optimal understanding of language also means that a primary tool and channel for learning (which language certainly is) is fluent and largely effortless. In rough terms of neural-resource accounting, knowledge will therefore both "cost less" to acquire, because reading and language generally are so easy, and the storage and maintenance of that knowledge will *also* cost less, due to the freed-up neural resources that can be utilized for memory of information and higher-level concepts. As I previously noted, as native readers become more common, and as neuroscientific research advances, it will be interesting to see if functional brain-imaging studies can someday directly detect the efficiency and compactness of native readers' neural representation of language, and perhaps even document the reallocation of freed-up resources for, say, foreign languages, musical ability, or mathematical skills.

(4) It is also possible that learning both spoken and written language simultaneously and early is beneficial because it amounts to the introduction of an important higher-order analogy early in intellectual development, and that this example may help develop a quite general talent for perceiving and constructing other complex analogies. This is important, as perceiving and constructing rigorous analogies arguably constitutes much of intelligence. By learning the isomorphism between the spoken and written word, early and at a low level, a child may gain a familiarity with, and a prototype for, analogy-building in general. The generalized ability may then be applied to *naturally see* the sort of analogies—such as those, say, between mathematics and music—that must be explicitly pointed out and *taught* to most people. The children who, with little instruction, effortlessly perceive such

analogies are the ones who seem "quick" and "bright" to a teacher. Something like this argument is already made in support of the early introduction of a second language: the argument is that learning a second language early in childhood often *augments* (rather than competes with) the development of the first language, too, by encouraging a more flexible and powerful and general understanding of language. Working with a second language provides rich opportunities, and some necessity, for developing higher-level concepts about language (or meta-level concepts, in the terminology of formal systems). A child thereby develops a more general and conceptually sophisticated ability with *all* language, so that more complex tasks, like developing an extensive vocabulary or mastering complex sentence structures, become easier in the *first* language, as well.

Again, these different mechanisms are not mutually exclusive; I expect that all of them play a part in native reading's support of early, and lifelong, intellectual development. The four mechanisms are also, by the way, listed in what I think is the approximate order of their relative importance. The full extent to which native reading promotes intellectual and academic achievement will not be known until reading natively becomes much more common than it is at present. I do know, anecdotally, that college-level mastery of essentially all aspects of language is attainable by the age of eight years. And this achievement was attained in an environment which, while I hope it is intellectually rich and emotionally supportive, is also a rather unstructured pedagogical milieu, to be perfectly honest, with almost none of the traditional discipline and focus that most people believe is necessary for this sort of achievement. The main "method" being what most would see as essentially just free time, or self-directed "play" (which can, of course, be a most powerful way to learn).

By the way, if you're reading this note and find this discussion overly technical, with all the references to isomorphism and formal systems and the like, remember not to worry over it. I put discussions like this—which are hopefully interesting for some people, but possibly annoyingly technical for others—into a separate section of notes because they are *not* essential to gaining a working understanding of native reading. The details of mapping and isomorphism which underlie the logic of native reading are not critical to fostering a rich native-reading environment for your child; just as understanding these same concepts is not critical to creating a rich enough environment to help a child learn to speak. The natural ability of children to implicitly perceive the isomorphisms of language constitutes much of their genius. They make use of these structural simplicities when they master language with miraculous rapidity and ease. Neither they nor their parents need to explicitly understand the abstract concept of, say, "isomorphism" in order to do this.

Remember, in order to catch a baseball you don't need to know how to explicitly write the parabolic equation for a projectile (including a complex correction for frictional energy loss). Such knowledge is also pretty useless when you are helping a child learn to catch a baseball. Given a rich enough environment, given enough practice and encouragement, children will learn to catch when they are ready. And they will learn this long before they ever encounter quadratic equations! (Of course, if they are native readers—given the timetable of the maturation of physical agility for most children—they will probably learn to skillfully catch a baseball long after they are reading chapter books on their own!)

page 47 *It may seem strange but—even for the express purpose of fostering reading—some of the books that you read to your child can be, and should be, books with only pictures!* Beyond the reasons in the main text, there is another reason that picture books can actually help children along in their reading, even after they have begun to pay attention to text and have started to make sense of it. This reason is that there will come a point where children *will notice that the text is missing* in their picture books.

Noticing that something's missing, or more generally noticing that something is wrong, can indicate an important cognitive threshold. It shows that a child has an internal model of reality, and that the child is confident enough in this model to make a genuine *judgement* about the world. If, for example, you find that one day your child is looking at *every* book upside down—not just looking randomly upside up or down, or even sideways— this not only shows that your child almost certainly understands the proper orientation, which he or she is *consistently* contravening, but that your child has, in fact, already moved a cognitive step beyond simply recognizing and following the rule. A child at this stage not only knows how things should be, but is also exploring how things should *not* be, and why.

In a similar vein, I was convinced that my daughter Freya truly understood the concept of counting on a particular day when we were driving in the car. She was about three-and-a-half years old. The windows were open and I had my new Feist CD blaring. The wonderful song "1234" was playing. To fit the lines into the 4/4 time, complete the rhyme, and to avoid seven—the only two-syllable digit—one lyrical couplet in the song is, "One, two, three, four, five, six, nine or ten / Money can't buy you back the love that you had then." Immediately after this line, Freya shouted from her car seat, "Hey, she forgot seven and eight!" Now, Freya had been counting beyond ten for well over a year at this point, but her quick recognition of another's "mistake" showed more evidence of understanding than did the simple habit of counting.

page 63 *Young children are extraordinarily adept at picking up complications and quirks of language and using them as if they were perfectly natural. Let them use their genius; don't shelter them from the complexity that they can handle particularly well at this age.* This ability young children have, to pick up and assimilate complexity, and to then see it as perfectly natural—to see right through the complexity, as it were—is an extraordinary skill. I think it results from that fact that earlier in childhood we have fewer cognitive preconceptions or prejudices. It is not a fluke that the irregular verbs in language tend to be the most common verbs—"to be", "to have", "to see", "to eat", for example—the very verbs which are encountered very often and very early in life. Very young children don't yet have a clear cognitive model of what a regular verb is, therefore they find irregular verbs quite natural early on, and they cognitively assimilate them with little difficulty. They have less to unlearn at this age. So the linguistic observation that the most common verbs, particularly those that are introduced early and often in child development, are also the most stable irregular linguistic complexi-ties—this structural feature of languages is developmentally based. So in many (even most?) languages the verb "to be" is irregular, while a more 'adult' verb like "to barter" is seldom so; "to eat" is, again, commonly irregular, but "to procrastinate" is generally not; and so on.

page 63 *This same approach to uppercase and lowercase letters [introducing them naturally] also applies more generally to the various fonts of printed words, and even to cursive. In general you shouldn't exaggerate the complexities, but you also shouldn't go out of your way to shelter your child from the natural diversity of the written word.* Children's prodigious ability to deal with different fonts and writing styles does not stand in isolation. It is mirrored in their equally amazing, but seldom commented on, ability to see through visual complexities of perspective, color, shading, and stylization as they learn to accurately identify classes of objects. For example, nearly every child quite rapidly and quickly learns to identify many common animals in a myriad of confusing "fonts": they learn to see cartoon pigs, fuzzy stuffed-animal pigs, simplified puzzle-piece pigs, and photographs of various pigs (seen from the side or the front, whether spotted or pink...) all as "pigs". Children's ability to successfully identify dogs, too—given the extreme variety of coat, color, form, and size that human breeders have come up with—is absolutely extraordinary. So the next time you see a toddler point at a chihuahua and say, "doggie!"—a scene so normal that few think to reflect on it—you should consider genuflecting before the genius to which you are witness.

page 70 *It's also important because music clearly helps structure memory. Many children who have difficulty memorizing phrases, or even short poems, nevertheless can recall many classic children's songs in their entirety, once they get going.* There is a downside to this importance of music to memory. It still pains me that once the melody starts in my mind, I can recall *every single word* of numerous songs from my teenage years and earlier; including many songs that I would much rather forget. I know I am not alone in this sort of thing. My brain is also littered with television advertisement jingles, theme songs, and now that I'm thinking of it—and, believe me, I *am* resisting—my horrible elementary-school alma mater (which the enthusiastic, but not especially gifted, school music teacher took it upon herself to compose) is positively *ringing* in my mind. *"University Hills! Rah, Rah, Rah! University Hills! Rah, Rah, Rah! University, University Hills!"* (Mrs. Kitchen, I would really like those neurons back please! Nostalgia aside, I could use them for much better purposes.)

page 77 *I believe that baby signing can be a great complement to native reading.* For those unfamiliar with baby signing, there are many books on the subject and numerous online resources, too. If you are interested, one good place to start is the book *Baby Signs: How to Talk with Your Baby Before Your Baby Can Talk* (by Linda Acredolo, Susan Goodwin, and Douglas Abrams; McGraw-Hill), which provides a useful introduction to the practice and motivation of baby signing.

page 79 *This does not mean that children won't eventually expand their reading ability by playing computer games, or by watching their favorite videos. They almost certainly will, if those things are to be found in your house.* Such things are found, in moderation, in my family's house. My children did watch an occasional video, and a small amount of noncommercial television while they were each learning to read (although they watched no more than a few hours per week, which from statistics I have seen, is nearly an *order of magnitude* less than the average child). I don't think this amount of selective TV viewing hurt their progress in reading. However, despite the attempts that the better PBS shows make to be truly educational, I'm not at all convinced that even the best television shows are terribly effective learning tools. I think parents shouldn't fool themselves into considering television as more than entertainment. As a learning medium, the inherent passivity of video—the lack of meaningful interactivity—is a fundamental drawback that is hard to overcome. This is particularly true for very young children (although not only for them!).

There is only one video that I believe might have actually helped my children in their progress as native readers: the children's video "Alphabet Soup", by the artist William Wegman. This video is a very simple, silly, and, for my children, at least, amusing trip through the alphabet. It displays an unusually consistent and straightforward correlation of the written and spoken language throughout most of the video. Plus there's just something about dogs dressed up as people that a two-year-old can uniquely appreciate. And talk about children's ability to understand unusual fonts—with this video they see the alphabet in many forms, including in the form of what amounts to "Wegman's Weimaraner Extra Bold" font: letters entirely made of imperturbable Weimaraner dogs.

In general, I believe that computer games, with their potential for meaningful interactivity, have many more redeeming characteristics than passive video watching. My children, for example, enjoyed playing the occasional simple children's game on the computer, and started doing this before they turned two. My daughter, in particular, sometimes seemed to prefer computer games to books. She liked the way she could control the action, in a way that's not possible with video, or with books for that matter. (This is consistent with the fact that, for quite a while, her favorite books were often lift-the-flap books, which are about as interactive as books get.) On the computer, Freya mastered the basic action of pointing and clicking with the mouse almost immediately. It was amazing how quickly she could navigate around a game, even maneuvering through the sort of menu hierarchies that can stymie many adults. Children are amazing at this. By learning to click on the "Play" and "Continue" and "Exit" buttons, a child is really *using* language, with the written word directly correlated to an action, and *the child's initiative* accomplishing the connection. This latter point is important, I think, because when the association is made by a child's action, that means the child's attention is necessarily focused on the correlated event at the exact time the event happens. Trying to do anything as effective with video is *much* more difficult.

However, while I do believe that occasional computer games were useful additions to their play, until my children were at least three years old they only enjoyed playing on the computer for very long if they were sitting in a parent's lap and *sharing* what they were doing. To be really engaged, children generally need social interactivity. Therefore, neither television nor computer games make good babysitters. In general I believe that—particularly in the first few years—children's interest in a computer game will be significantly correlated with *your* interest and attention while they play it. This is another instance of a child's important overall strategy of using *your* behavior to help decide what's important in the world, what's really worth exploring and learning. And always remember that children pay more attention to what you *do* than to what you *say*. If you say that playing on a computer is fun, but then ignore them while they do it, they lose interest. Similarly, if children see that you pay attention to them when they play with letters and read, their interest increases. Even when they see you read on your own, they'll often take notice and want to read themselves, if only in play at first. However, if reading is something you tell them to do on their own, while they see *you* talk on the telephone or watch television, children will get a clear message—and the message they'll get is not what you are *saying*, but what you are *doing*. If a child of someone who never reads ever does pick up a book, they may well start babbling into it like a phone. This is the reason I don't like the traditional "reading corner" to which children are exiled when they are supposed to read. Sure, sometimes a child will appreciate the peace and quiet, but, particularly for native readers learning at one and two years of age, I believe reading is far more success-fully taught as a *social* activity.

Notes to Chapter 5. Early Signs of Success, Seeing Your Child's Progress

page 81 *I do believe, however, that a plateau period [when outwardly obvious progress of understanding is not evident] actually often represents a very important time where the neural organization and consolidation of understanding is taking place—consolidation that is critical to further progress but which may not be obvious in external behavior.* That so much neural organization is going on "under the surface" is the general reason why I think it's important not to *push* children when they learn to read (or indeed, when they learn to do anything else, at least during these early years of intense and fundamental neural development). This is why you create the richly-correlative environment of native reading for children, but you then allow *them* to select, through their attention and enthusiasm, what they are ready to concentrate on. This allows their developing brain to focus on what are currently the most useful aspects of the environment for increasing understanding. This approach works for learning to talk in these first years, and for learning to crawl and then to walk, and it similarly is the best approach for native reading. A primary job of young children is to understand their world, and they are truly little geniuses at it. Let them set the pace. Encourage, but don't direct play. When reading, point at the text, but don't try to *make* a child look at it.

Like all geniuses, sometimes your child will show periods of less apparent interest, daydreamy days where he or she does not seem to be concentrating very well at all. This is to be expected. The brain does not just match input to appropriate output in a simplistic manner. If the mechanism of learning *were* so simplistic, then one might expect learning to correlate in a simple linear fashion with the amount of information the learner encounters. *If* that were the case, then simply pushing the rate of information encounter might yield the best rate of learning, the greatest rate of cognitive progress. But learning is not this simple, the brain must also *organize* its internal representation of the world and it does this by taking what it knows—its current internal representations—and reanalyzing and reorganizing this information. The digestion of new information is therefore not a simple one-time event. To take the alimentary analogy further, this consolidation of understanding represents a kind of intellectual chewing of the cud. (It is most appropriate that we use the word "ruminate" in exactly this sense.) In this process, remembered observations and experience, and tentative higher-level concepts—models of the world—are reanalyzed; they are compared to *other* observations and models, and the information is reorganized in order to advance higher-level conceptual understanding. As I conceive of it, in general and abstract terms, this process is one whereby the *isomorphisms* within the data of experience are ferreted out and, by creating analogies (or maps) between these isomorphic subsets, the process allows at least three important cognitive advancements:

(1) By minimizing redundancies inherent in isomorphic structures, the information of experience can be represented in the most compact manner; this compact representation allows the most efficient utilization of neural resources, and thereby maximizes the density of knowledge in the brain (which should also maximize overall intelligence, inasmuch as total cognitive resources are limited).

(2) With the neural representation of information organized and compact, the speed and efficiency of *access* to knowledge can also be increased. The location of functionally-related knowledge sets can be optimized so that memory recall and the general speed of mental performance are improved.

(3) Perhaps most important, by recognizing isomorphic structure in the environment, understanding can be extended through conceptual interpolation and extrapolation. A very simple example of this is how, once children become native readers—that is, once they understand and master the fairly simple mappings between the spoken language and the written language—they can begin to naturally use words in speech that they have encountered only in reading. And vice versa, too: from very early on they can easily read and comprehend many words the very first time they encounter them in written form. They can do this through a simple form of extrapolation, using the mapping of the written word to the analogous spoken word which they have previously encountered. Their comprehension then arises naturally through their experience with the social use of the spoken word. With a native reader's compact and efficient neural representation of both the written and spoken language, this experience translates beautifully into reading, even though no explicit definition of the word has ever been encountered.

I believe it is this mutual reinforcing of spoken and written language that makes native reading so powerful—not only for learning to read, but also for increasing the sophisticated understanding and use of spoken language, too. And, of course, a whole universe of specific and advanced subjects opens up for a child with well-developed language skills. When a child can read well and easily, it becomes easier to read *about* math, art, science, games, astronauts, animals, baseball cards, and a million other subjects. Understanding breeds understanding.

By the way, there is evidence that much of this important organization of experience, this intellectual chewing of the cud, may happen during sleep. "Sleeping on it", in fact, may often be good advice. (And "daydreaming" may be, functionally, an almost literal term.) Sleep's importance for learning would also be consistent with the fact that the proportion of each day we spend sleeping gradually decreases through life. It helps explain why infants and young children need to sleep so much, in fact for the *majority* of each day early in life. Otherwise being so sleepy would seem a strange strategy for learning—why give up so much waking experience?

page 85 *If you are not on the lookout for this behavior [a preference for right side up text orientation], it can be quite subtle, because the 'righting' of text is done naturally and even 'thoughtlessly' most of the time.* Although it can be subtle behaviorally, it's actually quite simple to nonintrusively determine whether children are viewing text in random orientation or not. Just give children ten unbiased opportunities, spaced out during a day, where you hand them a book, or a sheet of paper, or a notecard with their name written on it in bold letters, or anything else of the sort. Then note the way they choose to look at the text. If you're careful not to bias your presentation, the way they settle on viewing it each time is usually quite clear. Then you statistically take each trial as a coin flip (upside down or right side up). If a child chooses right side up 8 of the 10 times, there's less than a 5% chance that the result was a statistical fluke, and a 95% chance that this preference for right side up is real. If children do it correctly 9 times out of 10, the chance they "know what they are doing" is 99%. And if a child chooses right side up *every* time in ten, you can be 99.9% certain that this child is already solidly on the path towards native reading.

Variants of this sort of procedure are virtually endless: you can take a few minutes and carefully record the amount of time a child spends looking at letters in various orientations during letter play; or you could leave note cards with simple words on them in a room in random orientation, and record the direction from which a child approaches the card; or present cards with text right side up half the time and upside down half the time and note whether a child makes an effort to manipulate the upside down cards more often.

In addition to satisfying your own inner skeptic, this sort of thing can actually be fun to do—for you and for your child. Methods like this can also be useful to convince, say, your surly Uncle Ned, who insists that reading to a one-year-old child is an entirely worthless activity (if you judge it worthwhile to try to convince such a person). But, in practice, testing like this soon becomes superfluous. Just seeing your child making clear, neck-craning efforts to view a word in its proper orientation is quite unmistakable, given that there is really only one way to view it properly, and a multitude of random orientations that your child is clearly avoiding. But if you are a scientific sort, and if you do it in a way that feels natural and is fun for your child, I think it's entirely fine to put children to the occasional rigorous "test" like this. Done right, not only will young children *not* feel "tested", or in fact pressured in any way, but, if they notice anything at all, they will usually actually appreciate and enjoy the extra attention you're giving them. On the other hand, if you find yourself testing your child more than once or twice a month, there is a good chance that you *are* overdirecting your child's play. And always, the moment a child shows any aversion to the testing game, the subject should be dropped: use a child's enjoyment as your overriding guide.

page 89 *...you probably won't be able to resist a little test: you ask for the 'D' again [which your child correctly identified and retrieved, spontaneously, just earlier], probably directly this time. Your own eyes will be wide with anticipation as your child immediately plunges* both *hands into the pile of letters and, with the brightest of smiles, confidently presents you with* a 'Q' and a 'K'. My son made a similar sort of "mistake" after he first successfully read a word out of context. He and I were playing with play letters, assembling rhyming words. We were changing the first letter, and I was reading the words for him. I had done "CAT", "HAT" and "MAT" among others, and I then did words ending in "-OT". I assembled several words like "POT" and "NOT", pronouncing them myself, and then spelled the word "DOT". This time, before I had a chance to read it, Otto said himself, quite clearly and naturally: "Dot." He recognized a few favorite words at this point in his childhood—his own name, "Mama", and a few others—but "dot" was definitely not a word he was particularly familiar with. I asked him to say it again, and he again clearly said, "Dot." I still hadn't said the word myself. At this point I got pretty excited. It seemed undeniable that my son had just read his very first word! And he wasn't even 18 months old yet! (By the way, at this time I did not yet fully realize how different my methods of teaching reading were, in actual practice, from those of most other parents, so I was even more surprised at his early success than I am now. All the same, even at the time, his reading progressed in a manner that seemed perfectly natural and sensible to me; within a few months, and especially after my daughter read before three, too, the relevant question started to become, "Why don't most children read this early?")

So, back to the story: Otto had just read, twice, the word "Dot". He was not terribly familiar with the word "Dot", and he had not read it in the possibly-remembered context of a book he knew, but in the form of a novel word assembled in front of him. So I was excited. It seemed pretty unambiguous. Otto had picked up on my excitement by this point, and he was now grinning as he pointed at the word, he was dancing a little toddler jig, and he was shouting "Dot!" at the top of his voice.

I then changed the word, spelling something like "LOT". Otto smiled, pointed, and sang out...

"Dot!"

I tried to hide my disappointment. I spelled "GOT" for him.

"Dot!" he sang again.

Setting my teeth, I spelled "COT".

"Dot!" he shouted again, pointing at the word "Cot" and jumping up and down.

And so on. In fact, this comedy lasted for some time. For about a week, whenever we assembled words, he danced about and shouted, "Dot." However, all my years of scientific training still told me that it was pretty unlikely that the first success had been a complete fluke. To pick the correct "d" sound out of the thirtyish phonemes of English and to pronounce it so naturally—and to do this in his very first spontaneous attempt to pronounce an assembled word—well, this was not impossible to occur entirely by chance, but it was definitely *very* unlikely.

Given Otto's progress soon after this episode, I am quite sure his first reading of "Dot" was *not* a fluke. Otto soon stopped seeing nearly every assembled word as "Dot". This happened after only occasional and gentle correction during word play ("No, not 'dot', Otto, this word is 'cat', see? 'C' 'A' 'T'. Cat"). I didn't avoid his great enthusiasm for the word "dot"; in fact, I often humored him by ending a session of word-assembly play by actually spelling "dot" for him. This was always a hit. After just a few more weeks of native-reading play, of reading with text-pointing, of our other usual activities, my son was indeed pronouncing many words accurately and out of context. Within a few months, his ability to read independently was unmistakable.

In general, it's rather ironic that an important sign of success may, superficially, look at first rather like a new way of making mistakes. Again, there is such a thing as an intelligent mistake. I believe Otto had indeed made the important insight that novel words could be assembled from letters. I think he recognized his success, and this insight was considerably more important to him than getting the *correct* mapping from letters to sounds, from the written to the spoken word. He was mostly excited to have just perceived the mapping at all, not in getting it right. New knowledge always brings opportunities for new sorts of mistakes. This is why I believe one should always be careful to avoid spending a lot of time "correcting" a learner, or else the process becomes much less fun. I find this to be true, by the way, not only for a one-year-old learning to read, but also for a college student learning, say, evolutionary game theory. At first a little knowledge is a dangerous thing, but with more work, and especially through making mistakes and learning from them, real understanding and, eventually, fluency can result. This is also true when learning a foreign language; for myself at least, if I "correct" myself a great deal and, in general, if I let myself worry about making mistakes—constantly self-editing—I find that it really gets in the way of my fluency.

Notes to Chapter 6. Some Common Misconceptions About Native Reading

page 98 *We quickly found another preschool for our son, where his teachers were completely supportive of his early reading.* We ended up very happy with a Montessori school for our son and daughter. I'm not sure that our experience is easily translatable: every child, every teacher, and every school is different; you have to find the particular combination that works best for your family. Montessori practice, as I've encountered it anyway, does not particularly emphasize early reading. However, it doesn't seem to see early reading as either a philosophical or a practical problem, as some other early educators strangely do. I believe this is largely because Montessori emphasizes *diversity* in child development, and takes a positive view on individual variation. Because of this, I've found that Montessori teachers don't seem to teach exclusively to some hypothetical "average child". I feel that far too many schools mistakenly focus on the fictional "average child", either as a principle or as a lazy shortcut, to the great detriment of the diverse real children in the actual classroom.

In contrast, both Montessori philosophy and its methods allow and encourage teaching to the unique abilities of each child. This is greatly facilitated by the simple but important fact that a Montessori classroom is *not* a hub-and-spoke system where the teacher is the center of attention for nearly all activities. In a typical teacher-centered classroom, the students are often led through the same group activity at the same time and at the same pace. In such an environment having children at different ability levels is indeed a problem. If you teach to the average, advanced students will be bored, and, at the same time, struggling students may be left behind entirely. In contrast, Montessori students choose their own activities and then do these activities more or less independently. This means that it just isn't a practical problem to have a fluently reading three-year-old in the same class as a four-year-old who doesn't yet know the alphabet; both children can find an activity that is appropriate for them, which fosters the learning they each are capable of with their varying skills.

That Montessori schools generally have multiage classrooms is also a big help, both pedagogically and socially. For example, while your three-year-old may well be the only three-year-old in her class who can read, she is probably not the only student in the room who is reading, because there are also four, five, and even six-year-olds in the class. Therefore, your three-year-old will have classmates to trade books with, friends who can read her first notes, and your child's teachers will also be accustomed to having readers in the classroom, even if your child is, in fact, the first *three-year-old* reader they have encountered.

Given the natural variation between individuals, I believe that age is, in fact, generally a very poor proxy for ability. To me, it seems to be sheer laziness that leads many in education to focus so much on age. It's ironic too, because strict age-specific expectations, which I think are often intended to be leveling, actually end up making many traditional classrooms very competitive places indeed. They are often frustrating and ineffective for struggling students, while at the same time boring and ineffective for advanced students. And students of all levels compete for the attention of the teacher who is at the hub of most classroom activities. I think this sort of inefficient, competitive environment is hardly optimal, particularly in preschool and in the first few years of elementary school.

page 99 *While you don't need to be an unusual genius to read before three, I believe that being a native reader might make you more likely to <u>become</u> a genius. Because native readers gain language fluency earlier, more deeply, and in its written form—and because literacy is a fundamental tool for further intellectual growth—it's a fairly straightforward consequence that native reading will generally help a child <u>use</u> the skill of reading to learn many important and interesting things. And, like language itself, native readers will tend to learn these things, which reading makes accessible, earlier and more deeply, too.* It's definitely speculative, but I wonder if native reading could help explain the Flynn Effect, which is the observation that IQs have been fairly steadily and very significantly increasing over the many years since rigorous testing was started a few generations ago. The implication seems to be that today's children are actually quite a lot smarter than their parents were—and *much* smarter than their grandparents—at least in the ways that IQ tests measure. The effect is named after James Flynn, the intelligence researcher in New Zealand who first identified the curious effect.

Here's the outline of my (again, admittedly speculative) argument for how native reading may explain part of the Flynn Effect:

(1) Native reading, broadly viewed, is probably not an all-or-none phenomenon (although there are likely to be non-linear thresholds that may sometimes give at least a semblance of discrete classes of readers); rather, an earlier and more extensive introduction of written language will tend to make children's reading ability *more* native, even if they don't read as conspicuously early as do fully-native readers. Such *partially-native* readers will still get some of the benefits of native reading: they will tend to be more

fluent and effortless readers, their reading acquisition will tend to be a bit earlier in development, and their cognitive representation of reading will tend to be more efficient in its use of neural resources and thus more cognitively compact (see earlier notes for more detailed discussion of this idea).

(2) While fully-native reading is still quite rare, over the last hundred years the acquisition of reading has tended to become somewhat *more* native for the average child. Over the last few generations—driven by decreasing parental working hours, decreasing child:parent ratios (smaller family sizes), greater literacy and education of parents, and the increased and earlier emphasis on reading to young children and on early education generally— children have gradually become introduced earlier and more extensively to the written word than was true in the past. Therefore, reading has become *more* native over the years (though still far from optimally native for all but a very few).

(3) With cognitive compactness, efficiency, and precocity of reading, intelligence will tend to be enhanced because (a) compactness increases available neural resources for other intellectual skills, (b) efficiency and fluency of reading decreases the cost of further literacy-based intellectual development, (c) with precocity of reading, such literacy-based intellectual development can start earlier in life.

That's the outline of the argument. If this argument has some validity, then the societal benefits of fully-native reading might include a population that is, on average, more intelligent. It's actually not an easy task to find good, consistently-measured historical data, but I'm currently pursuing data to test the second premise of the argument: whether the age of reading acquisition has, in fact, come down over the last century. Then the question becomes whether the magnitude of this earlier acquisition correlates with the magnitude of measured intelligence increases. I also hope to determine whether the variation in age of reading acquisition—variation by region, nation, economic class, or ethnic classification—might help explain the persistent disparities that intelligence and achievement tests often still demonstrate. I believe that explaining this variation is of greater social importance than explaining the overall Flynn Effect. For example, I think it's likely that children in poorer and less-educated families may tend to have a later and less-extensive introduction to reading, and that these children might then be handicapped, possibly throughout their life, by their less-than-native reading skills.

If this is the case, native reading might offer a solution: learning to read earlier and natively, throughout our society, might significantly reduce the troubling and persistent educational inequities that plague us.

page 100 *I am not at all surprised by cases of famous and accomplished writers, moguls, mathematicians, and other "geniuses" who were, in fact, early readers. I think this observation is often the root of the misconception that you have to be a genius to read so young. In fact, when they first saw my young children read precociously, several different people have brought up the tale of Mozart reading and writing music at a very young age. My point is that while Mozart's genius might have, in part, led to his early musical literacy, it may also have been his early fluency reading and writing music that helped to* develop *his genius.* I want to again emphasize a fact that I believe should be obvious: children (and adults, too) display a great deal of natural variation. The variation between individuals is both from underlying genetic variation and also from being raised in different environments. This means that—to put it somewhat oxymoronically—in human development, as in practically all aspects of biology, exceptions are the rule. This is why I don't include a timetable for native reading development in this book; and this is why I'm not surprised by the different developmental trajectories of my own two children.

An appreciation of human variation is also why cases of late-talking geniuses like Einstein are not particularly surprising to me. I'm even quite open to the idea of Thomas Sowell (in his book, *Late-Talking Children*, already mentioned in a previous note) that some late-talking children—if I may put my interpretation on it to some extent—talk late because they have more difficulty with, or less interest in, the fairly complex and "fuzzy" mappings of natural language. But these same late talkers may have an unusually strong interest and ability with systems characterized by very *precise* mappings—systems like logic, science, mathematics, programming, and, perhaps, music.

I do, however, believe it's possible that some of these late-talking children might, in fact, speak earlier if they were raised as native readers. Their particular strengths with logically-rigorous systems might even make native reading work backwards for them, after a fashion. They might find the more formal system of the written language (without all the variation of intonation, volume, pitch, and the generally fuzzier colloquial usage that characterizes speech) to be a useful key to the otherwise baffling spoken language of their world. I still think the benefits of learning both the written and spoken forms of language simultaneously, where the understanding of one can reinforce the other, would generally be every bit as beneficial—even in cases like this, where the relative ease of learning to talk and learning to read might actually be reversed from what is considered normal.

By the way, I think the word "normal" is terribly misused generally, and I think it is an especially misused term in discussions of child development. Properly speaking, normal is not a point, it is an area: specifically, the area under the normal curve. Normal is a *distribution*, not an average. When many people, including many child development professionals, speak of the "normal child", what they are actually referring to is the "average child". The "average child" is an abstraction, and for many purposes it is a misguided and useless abstraction. Measure children in enough dimensions—height, weight, intelligence, creativity, agility, empathy, confidence, etc.—and you will soon find that no child is average.

page 103 *Misconception #3: If most children actually have the ability to read before the age of three, why do only very, very few children read that early now?* There is a more general objection some people have, particularly with regard to child-rearing and teaching, that is related to this misconception. I call this general objection "Pangloss's Fallacy", after the character Pangloss, the optimist fool of Voltaire's *Candide*. Pangloss insisted that the world was the best of all possible worlds. Put more simply, he insisted that everything is already perfect, or at least as good as possible. The version of this fallacy that gets applied to native reading is, "If it really were possible for children to read this early, it would already be common."

To counter this fallacy, you can start by remembering that near-universal literacy of *adults* has only become commonplace in the last hundred years, and generally only in developed countries. Until recently, the same Panglossian logic led many to believe that only the most intelligent people (by which they frequently meant, following the chauvinisms of the day, wealthy white men) were even *capable* of reading. As a scientist, I've always found it strange how many people succumb to Pangloss's Fallacy. Everything from automobiles, electric lights, airplanes, and telephones, to computers that can defeat humans at chess—among a million other examples—have clearly demonstrated that new ways of doing things can certainly succeed, despite the fact that people with little imagination initially found these things inconceivable.

I feel that susceptibility to Pangloss's Fallacy is at least partially explained by a severe limitation of imagination in many people. The mathematician and author George Simmons pointed out this limitation very nicely. While describing the profound and wide-ranging originality of the young Blaise Pascal, he struggled to express how truly unusual Pascal's mind was. He wrote, "There is a French saying that 'Many people know the whole history of human thought without ever having had one.' It is clearly true that most educated people in any period think other people's thoughts and little else. However, Pascal was trained by his father from infancy in the art of original thought, which is a rare and precious thing."

page 103 *In such a native-reading environment, however, I don't believe that recognizing text as meaningful is particularly hard for most children. Fundamentally, learning to read is not harder than learning to talk, it's just less intuitive.* It is not only because of my experience with my own children that I believe this; this assessment is also based on a general consideration of what is usually termed "computational complexity". Compared to learning speech, learning to read is simply not that hard computationally, particularly when it is learned right along with spoken language acquisition, or very soon after. To extend a facility with speech into the written word, all one has to do is learn a fairly simple mapping from sound to symbol (although the mapping is not as simple as one-to-one). Again, I believe that learning spoken language—with all its variation of pitch, intonation, volume, and pronunciation; some of which is meaningful, and some of which has no meaning at all—is actually, computationally, a harder problem than learning to read. The written word is the more "controlled" environment of language.

I am not mistaking the human brain for a general-purpose computer. For a general-purpose computer, computationally more difficult problems are necessarily harder to solve. This is not always true for the brain. The human brain is an artifact of our species' particular evolutionary history, and it has many cognitive constraints. This is why I believe children generally learn to talk without apparent effort, despite the computational difficulty of the task. We have an evolved ability to learn spoken languages, therefore we find the acquisition of oral language intuitive (at least when we are young). So we usually succeed in learning to speak without particular effort or intentional structuring of the learning process.

But perhaps the signal characteristic of the human brain is that it evolved sufficient cognitive flexibility to, in many cases, at least approximate a general-purpose computer. So, although such tasks were certainly not selectively significant during our evolutionary history, we nevertheless can learn to type on keyboards, drive cars, ski, surf, program computers, speak multiple unrelated languages, and solve differential equations. The computational power of our brain is sufficiently flexible to extend to these nonintuitive tasks quite well, particularly when we learn such skills at an early age.

Reading is also a novel and nonintuitive task; it is an innovation which is only recently to be found in our evolutionary history. We didn't "evolve to read." However, reading is deeply related to the complex but generally intuitive task of learning to speak, and the cognitive mapping necessary to extend language to the written word is actually quite computationally simple. So, with only rare exceptions, a child who can easily learn to talk (*i.e.*, nearly all children) and who is also capable of mastering nonintuitive intellectual tasks—for example, a child able to memorize all the Pokemon characters and their attributes, or able to recognize the many varieties of Barbie Dolls and remember their inter-relationships (and, again, nearly all children are capable of these things)—such a child must, therefore, possess the fundamental cognitive aptitude to extend his or her knowledge of language into the written word. What is lacking is the proper environment, not the ability. That is, given a sufficiently-correlative environment, where the mapping of spoken and written language is made plain, nearly all children can become native readers. And, while many children learn to read reasonably well later in life, in general the earlier they learn the better. If children learn early, they take full advantage of the brain's great flexibility during early childhood.

The decreasing flexibility of the brain, especially for "low-level" sensory and cognitive tasks, is almost certainly an adaptive trait. Once the environment has been "sampled" through experience for many years, there is a decreasing probability of encountering new fundamental things to learn. The more you know, the less likely it becomes that new knowledge will be worth the cost of both major cognitive reorganization and of outright reallocation of neural resources. The modern human environment, with its extraordinary technological and cultural complexity and with its constant innovation, certainly challenges this "evolutionary expectation" of decreasing environmental novelty. Dyslexics, I believe, are similarly challenged because they mastered the "low-level" features of language when they learned to speak—years before they encounter writing. When they start reading much later, their brains are unexpectedly confronted with an entirely new low-level medium for language. This is especially difficult because this new medium of reading and writing is perceived through a distinct sensory channel (sight versus sound) and the conventions of the written word also actually violate many important low-level cognitive rules for visual processing (rules like the one which says mirror-symmetry is usually meaningless and should generally be disregarded for most visual objects, particularly objects not in motion).

This formerly-adaptive resistance to cognitive reorganization as we age also helps to explain attitudes like that of a grandmother I know, who, in her own unambiguous words, has "decided to sit the computer age out." (Although, to be sure, many adults do find learning new things quite stimulating, at least once they get past their initial resistance. This might be because, while there may be an overall trajectory of decreasing neural flexibility as we age, challenging the brain by learning new things may provoke a more local, but functionally significant, facultative increase in cognitive reorganization. In some cases, such a local increase in reorganization may be adaptively coordinated with life history events. For example, there is evidence that women significantly reorganize their brains during and immediately after pregnancy, which may be an evolved response to prepare them for all the learning required of a new parent. In general, the notion that "learning new things keeps you young," may have a real neurobiological foundation.)

page 104 *In fact, computer scientists would be considered geniuses if their programs could acquire natural spoken language just half as successfully as the average child!* There are quite a few people who find the field of artificial intelligence threatening, with images of superhuman robots and supersmart computers often springing to mind. Many people find the whole AI endeavor somehow dehumanizing. But one of the interesting upshots of AI work is that as we attempt to make machines more intelligent, we have gained a new appreciation of how amazing human intelligence is (and an appreciation for the evolved intelligence of other animals, too). In trying to teach computers commonplace human skills, such as the ability to understand speech, we gain a new perspective on the genius of the average human child.

In particular, we have gained an insight into the often "implicit" nature of intelligence, which has greatly influenced my formulation of native reading and the specific techniques used to promote it. The implicit parts of intelligence are those aspects of intellect that we don't even notice most of the time. For example, when considering the idea of teaching a machine to understand speech, many people assume that the main problem is essentially one of developing the machine's vocabulary. As it turns out, simply distinguishing human speech from background noise, something we generally do with no thought at all, is a considerable problem to start with. Then there is the problem of distinguishing where one word begins and another ends. Such reliable speech recognition and parsing is not at all a trivial problem. It turns out that this sort of *implicit* intelligence makes up much of the knowledge necessary to understand speech. (Again, in contrast, the controlled environment of the written word is actually much simpler than speech.)

As I've mentioned, this insight—the great importance of implicit intelligence—influences many of the specific techniques of native reading. For example, it's not so important to explicitly teach children the particular meaning of words early in their development. Rather, the most important and rate-limiting step is helping children to realize that words simply exist, to realize that words are a meaningful part of their world. The particular meaning of words, at first, is quite beside the point.

The implicit nature of much of intelligence is also part of the motivation for the somewhat passive approach you use in teaching native reading. It's why you *promote* native reading more than you explicitly teach it. For example, text pointing while reading a book to a very young child, and *doing this whether or not the child is paying attention to the pointing*, seems strange to many people. But for a very young child the object is to set up correlations that make the meaningfulness of written words, and their relationship to speech, seem natural and apparent in a general sense. Trying to somehow force a child's attention onto this correlation is actually likely to be counterproductive. The social aspect of doing this can be distracting for young children, so that this extra effort will actually get in the way of their developing an implicit understanding of reading. If you try to teach more explicitly, the result will be that your child will focus on *you*, rather than concentrating on the language.

Even later, when teaching native reading to an older child, you are not trying to teach them how to successfully expend effort at reading. Instead, you are teaching them to read effortlessly, without making an explicit effort to turn their concentration to the task at all. A very simple, but typical, example helps illustrate this: you don't generally teach a child explicitly that (English) text is read from left-to-right, and from top-to-bottom, they just learn this implicitly by watching reading in early childhood. This is a simple but clear case of implicit intelligence: typically, children don't *know* that they know this fact about English. Often it's only when people encounter a language with different conventions, like Hebrew or Arabic, that they confront the fact that they have understood and acted on implicit knowledge about English for all these years. Of course, confronting this fact usually takes the form of thinking how *strange* it seems that anyone does it another way.

163

I believe this is exactly how native readers like my children generally see even baroque conventions like silent letters and other strange orthographic practices. They learned them so early—just as they learned to conjugate common irregular verbs in early speech—that they hardly even notice such conventions. Similarly, both my children could soon phonetically sound out words very accurately, but they very seldom actually needed to do it. The process of mapping from the alphabetical series, to the phonetic series, to the word, and to the word's meaning, was all so efficient that they had no need to *concentrate* on the mechanics of this process at all. In fact, their literacy is so deep, I don't believe they even *notice* the mechanics most of the time.

page 113   *Whether such a setting [an institutional childcare setting] can approach the outcome of the best parent-led teaching is something I am less sure of.* My skepticism is driven not only by the specific problems of organizing and implementing successful institutional childcare which is responsive enough to foster native reading, but also by more fundamental considerations that flow from a biological perspective on early child rearing. From an evolutionary perspective it's quite clear that a young child is probably predisposed to trust, and to learn better from, close relatives, with a particular focus on the mother, given the crucial nature of the mother-offspring bond for all mammals in early development.

This sort of trusting relationship may indeed be "transferable" to a great degree. There is evolutionary precedence, as it were, in that some other primates do make use of babysitters, although these babysitters are often still related members of a small social group. But such occasional babysitting does not approach the situation that's quite common for many children today. Children may spend *the majority of their waking hours* with unrelated caregivers. And in the collective environment of most institutional childcare, there is usually *nothing* truly analogous to the one-on-one care that a parent, or even a babysitter, can provide. Given that the primacy of the parent-child bond—at least the mother-child bond—was almost certainly a constant throughout human evolutionary history, there is every reason to expect that much of child development is designed to make use of this bond, to take it as a given. Therefore, there is also every reason to expect that there will be consequences and side effects on a child's development if you replace this reliable, consistent, one-on-one attention with diffuse attention in an institutional environment.

I'm certainly not saying that we ought to go back to the Stone Age; but I do believe we should seriously consider how some forms of modern child rearing may clash with the evolved expectations of infants and young children. I am *not* falling into some "naturalistic fallacy", where natural = good, in any simple sense. This should be obvious from the fact that this entire book is about reading, which is certainly an unnatural behavior, but which I also happen to think is one of humanity's great achievements. However, the point of this book is that learning this unnatural skill in *the most natural way possible* has great benefits.

There is still a great deal of extremism in much of the discussion of this general issue (often called, somewhat misleadingly, the "nature-nurture debate"). Personally, I believe that such extremism is highly counterproductive.

Notes to Chapter 7. Can Native Reading Prevent Dyslexia?

page 118 *Many other aspects of written English which are particular difficulties for many dyslexics are, similarly, other symmetries or near-symmetries of letters: for example, 'p' and 'q', another mirror symmetry; 'u' and 'n', a case of rotational symmetry; and 'n' and 'm' or 'v' and 'w', which display a variant of another type of symmetry usually called translational or iterative symmetry.* There is a wonderful, classic book on the subject of symmetry by the mathematician Hermann Weyl entitled, simply enough, *Symmetry* (Princeton University Press). It covers the fundamental concepts, touches on some applications, and also gives an accessible introduction to the abstract mathematical generalization of symmetry. Learning to see symmetries (or, in what may seem to be a contradiction—but isn't—learning to make use of symmetries while not actually noticing them) is an important part of intelligence. In general, symmetries represent opportunities for condensing sets of raw information into more powerful structures of edited information. Recognizing symmetries allows you to eliminate the redundancy of information. We often do this at a very low level, neurologically speaking. This low-level understanding helps explain the fact that many people, especially many artists, have a very well developed sense of symmetry and proportion (which is related to symmetry), but this sense is oftentimes entirely intuitive. Many visually-talented people have great difficulty when they try to explicitly explain what it is that makes something "right" or "wrong". Good artists can see clearly what is visually pleasing, and they can use this vision to guide their construction of beautiful things, but they frequently have great difficulty explaining precisely how they do this, and difficulty in teaching others to do this. When artists do successfully teach, it's often indirectly—by example, or by supervising trial and error practice—rather than by explicit and precise instruction in the way that, say, a mathematician generally teaches. (Of course, because a great deal of intelligence is intuitive, or *implicit*, rather than explicit—and explicit knowledge is exactly what math and science try to achieve—many people actually prefer the oblique instruction of their art teacher to the explicit and logically rigorous instruction of their math teacher.)

page 120 *Children certainly vary, both in the timing of their optimal window for language acquisition, and in the length and shape of this developmental window of best opportunity.* The shape of a developmental window is probably best conceptualized as a probabilistic benefit-to-cost function through developmental time. This function may be sufficiently complex and graded in form so that the common term "window" is somewhat misleading. The window may be fuzzy, rather than discrete. But even if a developmental window is not absolute—as the term "critical period" is generally taken to imply—it can still be an important developmental constraint.

For example, it's not that you *cannot* learn a foreign language when you're older. It is certainly possible for most people. But when older people try to learn a new language they often find that they have to work harder, while progressing more slowly, than younger people do. Because there is enormous genetic and environmental variation, there will always be rare exceptions to this rule—there will be an occasional adult who learns more easily than a particular slow-learning adolescent—but the rule still holds, probabilistically, as such cases will be relatively rare. A more accurate, but cumbersome, way of describing a window of opportunity might be to say there is an optimum time to learn, but then to remember that there is an associated probabilistic function describing the way the benefit-to-cost ratio decreases as you get farther from the optimum.

A reasonable objection to the term "window" is that it implies that it is futile for an individual who is past that window to try to learn a task later in life. That interpretation is indeed misleading in many cases. But, in other cases, developmental windows may indeed approach the usual definition of a "critical period". Some windows, at least for some individuals, may be sufficiently discrete that, once one is past the window, the opportunity is truly lost. For example, some low-level features of language, like the ability to speak without a discernable foreign accent, are extremely hard for nearly *all* adults to master, and sometimes impossible—while children typically learn these things easily.

So the native-reading theory of dyslexia proposes that many dyslexics are children who were simply introduced to written language too late. Their window of opportunity for learning language fundamentals was far past its optimum. For some varieties of dyslexia, the problem may lie primarily within now-inflexible visual processing itself; in other cases the problem may be in linking *visual* sensory data with an already well-developed language center that is richly-connected to *auditory* processing in the brain. But while details certainly vary, in general the problem is that neural flexibility for learning low-level language mechanics was greatly reduced by the time these children were given the opportunity to learn to read. Again, in most cases, dyslexic children can make significant progress even late in childhood—the benefit-to-cost ratio has not usually gone to zero—but progress will be slower, harder work, and more frustrating than if they had learned to read nearer to a child's optimal time for acquiring the fundamentals of language.

Notes to Chapter 8. What Native Reading Will Give to Your Child

page 124 *These [late reading] children are working hard, and they are often very intelligent; the problem is that their intelligence is largely focused on the* mechanics *of the written word. If only they had learned to read earlier, not only would they have mastered these mechanics long before school, but the quirky mechanics of writing would generally be something that they* would not even notice. I have a great deal of sympathy for this struggle because it is very much the same struggle I have when I attempt to read music. My problem is that I only learned to play piano, and to read music, when I was thirty years old. Despite considerable effort over many years now, I still have no real fluency when reading music. My attempts remain halting and frustrating. It takes so much effort for me to deal with the mechanics of musical notation—to remember exactly which note each line on a staff represents, what all the little flags and rests mean, to follow the part for each hand on the two different staffs, especially when the melody occasionally jumps from the bass to the treble and back—that I can sometimes find it very hard to keep the flow of the music going. In fact, I often simply can't. For a piece of any complexity I have to learn it first by picking my way through it slowly and laboriously. I am like a poor reader sounding out Shakespeare phoneti-cally. Only after months of this effort, after I've essentially memorized the piece, can I begin to play it fluently and with feeling. My need to memorize works before I can enjoyably play them terribly limits my repertoire. I'm very envious of those who learned to read music early and who are therefore deeply fluent.

page 124 *But many more poor children are left to struggle with a very non-native facility with the written word, sometimes for their entire lives. They therefore suffer more frequently and more severely from dyslexia and from other language-based learning disabilities. Even much later in their schooling, these children tend to find reading and learning much more work, and much less rewarding, in comparison to children who were early readers.* As I've empha-sized elsewhere, windows of development are generally not discrete, all-or-none, phenomena. Also, there will always be occasional exceptions to these sorts of generalizations, due to variation among individuals in both aptitude and in social support for literacy. However, in general, I expect that children who are introduced *earlier* to reading will have a *more* native understanding of the written word, even when it falls far short of fully-native reading. As it stands now, I think that many children from the least literate and educa-tionally-supportive homes—who then often go on to some of the least effective schools, too—are introduced so late to reading that they may suffer from an extremely non-native grasp of written language. I believe that this may frequently persist as a lifelong handicap, and that it may be a primary explanation for later educational underperformance, even as late as college and beyond. As I've detailed in Chapter 7, I think that this can take the form of profound dyslexia, and that this dyslexia is often *caused* by learning to read too late. (*Not* the other way around, *not* that dyslexia caused them to read late; at least for many cases.)

I am not saying that it is *impossible* to "make up" for the delayed intro-duction of reading through intensive efforts in later education. (I do, however, fear that such remediation may indeed prove impossible for *some* individuals, specifically those individuals whose neural flexibility for acquiring low-level language decreases faster than in others.) But I think a more effective and profound improvement in educational equity might be made by stopping the problem at its source—by someday providing *all* children with deep and effortless literacy through native reading.

page 125 *I am aware that, in the short term, the introduction of native reading is unlikely to noticeably decrease educational inequity. To start with, the early adopters of native reading will be those parents who have the time and the inclination to read a book like this. Such parents are likely to be more literate, more educated, and, if not necessarily wealthy, still probably less likely to be extremely poor.* I'm happy for every child who benefits from native reading, but I also think it is important to take an active role to help make native reading available to everyone. This is especially important because those children whose parents are less likely to be early adopters of native reading probably have the most to gain from it. I am, therefore, very interested in the possibility of establishing a pilot preschool, with an associated parent-education program, in order to demonstrate the effectiveness of native reading for economically-disadvantaged children. I hope that such a demonstration project would not only be of great benefit for the children enrolled, but that it would also clearly demonstrate the enormous benefits we could gain as a society if we did a better job of harnessing the genius all young children have for learning language. A successful demonstration would also provide a clear sense of the societal cost we pay by largely missing this opportunity now, particularly for poor children.

This would not be a small undertaking, and I don't have the resources to carry out such a project on my own. Therefore, if any educational researchers, foundation trustees, or private individuals with the means and the inclination to fund such an effort are reading this—if they find themselves similarly excited by the opportunities that native reading could provide for children from all backgrounds—please get in touch with me and let's get started (tim@nativereading.com).

Acknowledgements

M any people and places are responsible for the intellectual background that prepared me to see the possibility of native reading. Among these influences were many of my professors at Earlham College, especially Peter Suber—he is the person who introduced me to logic, programming, and artificial intelligence, and he taught me a great deal about creativity and human intelligence in the process. I also benefited from many of the scientists I worked with and around during my graduate studies at Princeton University. Also, not long before the birth of my first child, I had the opportunity to give a talk at The Neurosciences Institute. I found my visit there quite inspiring, and I learned a great deal about neuroscience from Gerald Edelman and his coworkers. Their models of human cognition were often on my mind when, soon, I found myself watching my children learn to make sense of their world. Also, though I first read it very long ago, Douglas Hofstadter's book *Gödel, Escher, Bach: An Eternal Golden Braid* has had great influence on my subsequent thinking about the foundations of intelligence, and about cognition generally. It is a wonderful, thought-provoking book. Most of these influences are highly indirect—none of them specifically involve reading acquisition, and few of them even touch on child development, at least not directly—but they nevertheless had a profound effect on me, and on this book.

By far the most critical people for formulating these ideas were the wonders right in front of me. It was the amazing development of my own children, Otto and Freya, that inspired, informed and provided the first examples of native reading. They continue to inspire and delight me as they grow up all too fast. This book would never have happened without them. Their mother, Binney, my partner in life and a fellow scientist, has also been of the greatest importance in helping me develop the ideas and techniques of native reading. Many of the ideas in this book were first discussed with her; far too often these discussions were late at night, when the kids were finally asleep, and when she had the disadvantage of needing to wake up earlier the next day than I did. Her indulgence is much appreciated. Her mix of criticism and support helped give the ideas of native reading their final form. I'm also grateful for her reading and critique of an early draft of this book and for her later help and advice with final book design.

Finally, I want to again emphasize that every child is unique and miraculous, and while I believe that most children can become native readers as mine did—if they are given the right environment—I would never expect your experience with your children to be identical with my own. Indeed, as I make clear in this book, my experiences teaching native reading to my own two children were quite different, while entirely successful in each case. The way in which every child is different, and yet there are commonalities they all share, is of great interest to me. I am, therefore, very interested in hearing about your experiences with native reading. To facilitate this, I've done that most modern of things: I've created a website. I invite you to share with me how these methods work for you and your child (tim@nativereading.com).

Biographical Note

Timothy Kailing grew up in Michigan. He was an undergraduate at Earlham College, and received his graduate degree from Princeton University, where he was a National Science Foundation Graduate Research Fellow. He and his partner raised their two children first in central Vermont, and now in southwest Michigan, where he also writes, teaches, and continues his research. He also is occasionally known to catch a trout.

Made in the USA
Middletown, DE
27 March 2016